P's giTa

ScriPTures
for
the
Now

ॐ श्री गणेषाय नम:

ॐ Shri Ganeshaye Namah

ॐ श्री दुर्गा महादेवी जगढम्बाय नम:

ॐ Shri Durga MahaDevi Jagadambaye Namah

Prashant Trivedi
PT The Axis

www.lotus-ocean.net
www.youtube.com/lotusocean

PT's Log

ScriPTures
for the Now

Setting the Record Straight

The ScripTures

Basic Definitions

Observations in this Matrix

Friends & Family

Sound & Music

Learning & Education

Spirituality & Evolution

Right Behaviour

PT the Axis

The ScriPTures

Real Revealed

in the Beginning arises the dot
the dot moves to create an arc (golden mean spiral!)
one becomes two
static & kinetic, Shiv & Shakti
three arcs are created with the dot in the center
Trinity is established
Multi-verse is born

AEIOUM is thus the symbol of creation
called Om or Aum when true knowledge is lost
amongst children of earth
every vowel is part of the play ...

ॐ CropCircle on 7.7.7 ~ Prashant Trivedi
youtu.be/mXcgPhkf8B4

the Name

whats in a name ?

not much considering the number of
johns & davids there are
in this world

it is just an 'identity tag'
which you unfortunately have to share
with many others

but if one looks deeper a 'name' might turn
out to be more than that
it might reveal one's function within
the bigger scheme of things

no i am not talking about numerology
even though that is also a good starting point
to discover the workings of multiversal functionings

for example going into the basics of yours truly's name
we discover ~
Prashant (pronounced Praha - shant with a soft 't' at the end)
Trivedi (pronounced Tri-vaidi with a soft d)
actual Sanskrit ~
Pra-shant = (Pra) Very (Shant) Peaceful
Pra-shant is thus also the sanskrit equivalent of Pacific (Peacefic)

Rainbow PrinTs the real Avatar's name in sky ~ Real Rainbow Bridge
<u>youtu.be/2ig3raR5X68</u>

Prashant @ Prashant Mahasagar (Pacific)

Himalayan PT ReSounding ... Real-Time Peaks Revealing ...
Shiv-Snow-Sonic-Alchemy youtu.be/hlzbOTD36j8

also

Praha - shant = Waves + Peace = Wave Resolution

nondestructive interference amongst waves

leading to superluminal faster than light implosion

Tri-vedi = 3 Vedas or 3 Main Systems of knowledge

also known as the 3 IDS or the 3 MEs

if you look at it in an Egyptian sensibility ~

P = Virgo = Mercury = Hermes

Tri-vedi is the same Tri-smestigus

so P Trivedi becomes Hermes Trismestigus

my initials PT become root of PTAH etc

which in its sanskrit root is Pitah, meaning father

or Patih meaning husband

P = Proper

T = Crossing

PT Skywalker sounds fine too in a birdtribe context

also,

P = Axis

T = Turning

to sum it up i like to say,

P is the P-ole you spin around

what was lost is now being found

the Real Stairway to Heaven/ Bliss/Enlightenment

since many have been asking
i felt it best to make this public
these are the 4 basic disciplines required to get the
MIND BODY SOUL DNA MATRIX
to generate bliss from within ~

1. RIGHT DIET:

Avoiding violent foods like meat &
bliss reducing ones like white sugar &
genetically modified foods

Recommended: Veggies, lentils, grains, nuts,
roots, herbs, spices ...

2. FRACTAL LIVING ENVIRONMENT:

Avoiding big cities, metal/concrete buildings,
power lines, mobile towers etc

Recommended: Old properly braided landscapes,
oceanside, old growth forests
(a tree is a fractal; ever wonder why Buddh got
enlightenment under an old tree),
phi based architecture, using biology friendly
building materials like granite,
bamboo, hemp etc

3. SHAREABLE THOUGHTS:

Maximizing thoughts which can be shared with anyone;
eliminates need for secrets and storage;
Zero storage = Infinite Connectivity;
thoughts which relate to Pure Principles
of the Universe - Like the patterns of
nature functionings, sacred geometry etc

4. COHERENT EMOTIONS:

E-motions (energy in motion) directed to
gene-rate-ing Compassion (complete passion) ...
emotions which reach beyond the
normal realm of negativity, sadness and despair or
momentary joy, happiness ...
emotions which can connect one to say
a tree, cloud and in due course a star ...
galactic emotions ... emotions which are like a laser
instead of a torchlight (laser travels
much farther because of its Coherence) ...

sorted multiversal emotions beyond
everyday pettiness which engulfs majority
of human lives

now the most important bit ~

there should be REAL HUMIILTY
towards the benevolent higher beings
which are closer to the state of PERFECTION than one is
this automatically allows for smooth EVOLUTION

the real journey only begins
after one has attained proper humility ...

The Four Pronged Approach

He who knows not,
and knows not that he knows not,
is a fool – shun him.

He who knows not,
and knows that he knows not,
is a child – teach him.

He who knows,
and knows not that he knows,
is asleep – wake him.

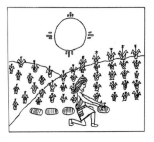

He who knows,
and knows that he knows,
is wise – follow him.

Basic Definitions

divine defined

one may ask
what is 'divine' ?
as we are communicating in english
we have to use the word
'divine' which simply translates to
di-vine or
'perfect branching'
because it comes closest to the
characteristics of *'paramatman'* – a sanskrit term
'god' is too loaded a word
mostly with misconceptions
also it is a male term while
divine is beyond male-female polarity

even though *'paramatman'* or divine
is beyond the realm of words
the simplest definition is –

the original creative spark which
despite having created
all the creations & dimensions
lies outside of it ALL

divine supports & encompasses all good
real love, peace, harmony, non-violence, painlessness etc.
many of the innumerable
qualities of divine like

perfection on all levels
are well documented in
vedic texts like the
puranas, ramayan, mahabharat etc.

divine = perfect fractality & perfect coherence
what these are cannot be understood
without a personal experience
through divine's grace

in the present time, space, realm, world
PT avatar
is providing a glimpse
into this fractality, coherence & synchronicity
through realtime
sound & light events
www.youtube.com/lotusocean

as long as beings stay
humble to the divine
there is no pain or torture

evil is born the moment any being
rebels against the divine
this rebellion arises
simply from wanting
praise for itself which it does not deserve

its elementary my dear ...

after severe disconnection from nature
& creating a plasticky concretey blissless world
people's definition of divinity
doesn't carry
connection with elements

when
divinity is / has always been / always will be
all about connection and manifestation
through elements

there is a reason why
the elementals are the *devas* (demigods)
the good guys / the real goodfellas
in vedic wisdom
agni (phire deity), *vayu* (wind deity), *varun* (water deity)
their head being *indra* (wielder of thunderbolt)
their mother being *aditi* (sky deity – the 5th element)
their support being *prithvi* (earth deity)

the body is made up of these elements only
& the soul ascends to higher realms
only after purification of the elements

element is elementary

the devas are always in heaven
only because they
always bow to the source – divine

16

higher & lower

in a world where equality
is a mass slogan
propagated by evil's minions
applied to gender, race, beings etc
and
higher/lower
are seen as swearwords

lotusocean declares
that there is higher and lower

the definition of
a higher being
is quite simple
'a being is higher than oneself
if the being is more connected to the divine than one is'

regarding
how will we gno etc.
it is very clear within the first instant
to those that are honest

if one doesn't gno how to behave properly
with a higher being
one has no chance of progressing towards the
eternal delicious overwhelming bliss that is divine

bliss

people ask
what is bliss ?

bliss is DNA on phire going past speed of light
bliss is kundalini going through the crown chakra
bliss is all the chakras flowering like lotuses
bliss is ability to steer one's soul after death
bliss is creating a rainbow at will
bliss is the brain on ecstasy through kundalini juices
bliss is surfing time without ever falling
bliss is to have one's fate completely in one's own hand
bliss is the ability to play with the elements

...

this is just a little taste of bliss
it is many more such things which most cannot even fathom

no pill, alcohol, drink, drugs, relationships,
self-guided diet, meditation or yoga
can give it

only way is
learning from those who have it
by bowing/serving

truth

truth
is the most misunderstood term
in muggle world

it is usually equated with
being accurate about
how many toffees one ate
how many apples one stole
how much tax one avoided
the unending information on forms
or other such useless petty trivia
meant for upholding the unholy system

krishn who always denied eating the butter
would be considered a liar
under current definitions
which people like gandhi have propagated

real truth as in
सत्यम शिवम् सुन्दरम
'satyam shivam sundaram'
meaning
'truth is shiv is beauty'
has nothing to do with
anything to do with this artificially created
society & structure
& its banal matters

real truth

is more to do with

seeing reality as is

without any distortion

truth is facing the reality of one's own being

and the lack of happiness therein

truth is in the laws of nature & divine

which are pure scientifically verifiable principles

not subject to change in time

truth is that divine exists

truth is that happiness can only exist

where/when divine is praised

honesty

honesty is another one of the many
important words
twisted beyond recognition
honesty has nothing to do with
not stealing bread and jam from the supermarket
or paying your bills on time
or not lying about the cookies you ate

honesty is actually about
being straight about one's state

honesty is about getting to the point
without this real honesty
one cannot hope to evolve

it is the first step
on the ladder out of hell

honesty allows one to seek the divine
or something higher than oneself to
help one out

it is said that
there are many confused people out there
what i would say is that
there are many dishonest people out there

impressed

impressed
means
'i am pressed'
i.e
being pressed enough to act

so one is not really
impressed
unless
one cannot help but act

many here
are impressed by
many things & beings
mostly at their own level or lower

but not many are
impressed
by divine
or real beauty

if they were
one won't miss it
as there would be
lots of actions
witnessed
in that direction

sincere

there are those
who are telling me
that a 'thankyou'
not followed by
any corresponding actual actions
can be sincere

i however find
people lining up outside night clubs
in freezing cold
some in miniminiskirts
sincere
for what one really wants to do
one dedicates time & energy
& goes to any length

real sincerity only exists
in
relation to that
which makes people act without restraint

simples

responsibility

the real meaning of the term

'responsibility'

is hidden by its spell-ing

its actually made up of 2 words –

response ability

yes

the ability to respond

promptly & properly

to higher & divine

is

anyone's

only

responsibility

this real responsibility

raises one up

instead of

weighing one down

any other sense

of it

will only bring one down

genesnakes

what are called humans in mugglespeak
are 'genesnakes' in lotusoceanspeak
even though the diversity seems mindboggling
there are not many of them here
a gathering
comprising of a single representative
from each one
would barely fill up a school hall

muggle

muggle is a term that is used
repeatedly in
lotusocean blogs
so its best to throw some light on it
a muggle
as now many children gno
courtesy the hari-putra (harry potter) books
is simply a non-magic person
i.e someone completely unaware
of the greater realities beyond
the 3d physical matrix
muggle is basically a being
who accepts the 3-d prison reality
as the only reality
and spends its time
continuously creating & dealing with petty problems
it goes under many pseudonyms
average joe, simple person, mass, mob, dude, bloke
it desperately tries to eek out happiness
in domains which don't have any
it defies divine
& creates tailormade gods suited to its own narrowmindedness
it has opinions
but no gnowledge
it has thoughts
but no clarity
it is theoretically awake
but practically asleep
it has fear
but no real curiosity
it has questions
but does not want any answers

White

just a quick observation on the
terminology assigned to a particular
race/tribe on this planet
the race/tribe termed 'white'
is not really 'white'
might come as a surprise to some
but those who have doubts
are advised to take a look at the colour
white
(over & over if required)
the so called white race is
actually more translucent
than anything else
reason being
lack of pigmentation
a disease called albinism
the complexion varies from yellow to red
skin is usually ruddy, pimply & scaly
the translucents is a more apt term
to describe this race/tribe
the colour white conjures up ideals
of purity & righteousness which are
erroneously ascribed by the subconscious to this
particular race through this false terminology

so much for the black & white
chessboard world which has been created
by those whose objective is to confuse

ps. though these words might rub some
people the wrong way,
it must be stated that
this blog is not here to promote racism
but as an exercise in seeing/naming things
as they are

Vegetarianism

there is general thinking/consensus
all over the planet
that not eating animal flesh is
vegetarianism
so the so-called vegetarians
have no qualms about having non-veg partners
even in nature
the herbivores & carnivores don't mate
horses don't mate with lions,
elephants don't mate with cats & so forth
but homo sapiens seemingly can override all natural law &
discomfort/awkwardness of nonsensical situations

they also freely go to discotheques, raves, trance parties, festivals
in the blessed comfort of gnoing that they
are vegetarians & thus against slaughterhouses &
animal cruelty & so forth
the simple fact that the techno music
they are enjoying is no different from
slaughterhouse machine sounds doesn't
cross their mind
also most of the
vocal music they hear is nothing
but the agonized cries of dying animals
channeled through homo sapien mouths

there is no realization that
vegetarianism is a whole way of life
not just a food choice
the whole gambit of meat, alcohol,
borgness, corpiness, non-veg company,
non-veg sounds has to be given up
together before one truly becomes a
vegetarian
the incomplete compartmentalized form of
vegetarianism is neither lasting
nor does it bring all the benefits associated
with vegetarianism
veg food + nonveg life = speedy disintegration

evol-love

the word love
keeps on getting used on this planet
a trillion times a day
without a clue as
to what it is

an extensive air of mystery
has been
created around a simple concept

to love someone
means that
you want the best for them
and the best that can happen to
anyone
is that they evolve
from their current state

to want evolution of anyone
is loving them
to want evolution of everyone
is loving everyone

the real spelling of evolve
evol-love
reveals its
absolute connection to
love

free to Phree

free
another word like 'love'
thrown around by people
without any proper understanding

so much pain, heartache & break arises
from the misuse of these key words

free has nothing to do with
doing whatever one pleases
or having all the money in the world

free = phi-ree = phi recursive =
phi rotation
at faster than light speed
which gives an ability to switch dimensions

in simple terms
it is ability to take the soul to higher realms
after death

real freedom has always been
freedom from
pain/torture of lower realms
& cycles of birth & death therein

complete freedom =
ascension to the highest realm of divine

unnecessary

majority of the real souls
on this planet don't like their job
repetitive boring tiring robotic

one cannot blame them coz
the simple truth is that
99% of the activities and jobs
on this planet
are **unnecessary**

unnecessary coz
they are not necessary
for
basic survival
or
evolution
and besides these 2
there is no other reason
for any other activity

evil is nothing but
the propagation of this
unnecessariness
to continually distract from
divine & evolution

ego

ego

is

simply

the

false

gnoing

within one

masquerading

as

real gnoing

ignorance + lie (that one gnos)

=

ego

which

in-turn

leads to

a

non-learning

attitude

which

in-turn leads

to bad things

happening to one

called

hell

way out –

to stop lying

about one's

gnoing

&

simply admitting that

one does not

gno

&

start learning

e-go

energy needs somewhere to go

with gnoing it can go

out of hell

into

heaven and beyond

...

selfish?!

its funny how
so many in this world
try so hard to be selfish
its always
me before you
but somehow they
never do their self any good
by their actions

if they were truly self-ish
they would improve their self
give it more strength
through evolving it
instead they bring their self
down to hell
by their foolish actions

so

they are not
really selfish
just plain foolish

even though self-ish is
a bad word in this world
it would be a welcome change
for them to
actually care about their
self
coz if they do
they will automatically care
about nature, right behaviour ...

insanity

this planet

resembles an insane asylum

more than anything else

because the people here

have made up

(in order to appear sane)

a whole lot of definitions

of insanity

while completely disregarding

the only real definition

–

all those

who do not want to

get out of hell and hellish conditions

3-d matrix

cycle of birth and death

are

insane

by

divine

certification

oPinion

only those who
have activated their pine cone pinion
in the pineal (3rd eye)
are entitled to
an
opinion
o-pine on and on
the rest just need to listen

emotion

e-motion

is

energy in motion

energy which seeks answers & ascension

& doesn't stop till it gets them

it can not be distracted

emotion has nothing to do with

all the senseless drama and crying

which happens in the muggle-world

a being who

after being born in human form

doesn't seek enlightenment

is a being

without any real emotion

a being with real emotion

can/will never serve

the evil system

nor can it be caged/trapped by

any of their devices

bowing to higher & divine

is the only way to inculcate

real emotion

divine's avatar intent

do you think
GoD/divine manifests
on earth in flesh & blood to
listen to your sins
cries for forgiveness
demands for this & that

no the divine
comes down
simply to
Play
& see who is willing to Play

within its divine parameters of course

thats the one & only judgement

the age old question

what are beings created for ?

a question that boggles many many minds & hearts

the answer as always is quite simple

beings are created for Playing with
the Original Creator
the Divine

on divine's terms of course

evil was nothing but
a refusal to Play
with the divine
on divine's terms
hells, pain, torture & infinite boredom
was / is the outcome
of that refusal

life

is

but

a

preparation

for

afterlife

not

many

understand

this

thus

all

the

mess

Observations
in this Matrix

prison/matrix

one has to gno
one is in a prison
before one makes
any attempt to escape

reality as it is

most people here

refuse (blatantly a lot of times)

to

see

reality

as it is

...

no wonder

they are trapped here

in this

prison

existence

&

cant get out

...

hello

all one hears is

hello

hello

yes we gno

hell is low

and

you are in it

no need to reiterate it

like a divine mantra

billion times a day

hi

the most prevalent greeting
of what is now called 'the west'
'hi'
pronounced 'haai'
is the same as a
hindi/urdu term 'हाय'
which means 'a call in/of distress'
makes sense
considering
that this is an actual reflection of their state
things have a way of giving themselves away
even if it is not intended that way

or are they trying to say
that the person they are addressing is
hi(gh)
or higher than them
if that is the case
their body language doesn't suggest
any such intent

all is well ?!

there are
those here who profess
all is well
and label anyone
who doesn't agree
as mad
yes
only earth is getting pillaged
animals bred & slaughtered in
cages smaller than their size
pollution is reaching
hypertoxic levels
there is no ground
remaining to be used as
a sacred space
beings are continuously
harming themselves, each other
and all the animal life
out of ignorance and evil
majority is on
a devoluting path
losing their soul every second
in an industrial-technological nightmare
everything is becoming borg robotic soulless
surely
all is well
no need for wholesale
drastic changes
from top to the bottom

happy ?

happy
a hyper used word in world today

everyone wants
to be
happy

without gnoing anything
in hellish conditions
without any proper actions

basically
baselessly
happy

of course
there is no such thing possible
so they just go on pretending instead
sticking their teeth out like mad beings

in a civilization
where people were actually evolving
and caring about their future
am sure
the word happy would hardly get a mention
as
beings would actually be in a bliss state

fun

the term 'fun'
is brandished around hell a lot
not surprising
as there is
a major lack of it

'lets have fun'
they say
in this hellish world they have created
as if fun is even possible in hell

its like asking an animal in a slaughterhouse
to have fun

only real fun (phun)
activity possible in hell
can be getting out of hell
&
that happens thru
praise/service of higher/divine

good & happy

there are too many

out here

who in order to justify

their jumping into the mad circus

label

fellow beings as

good

or/and

happy

well there is some news for them

as

no one no one

who is stuck out here

can be

neither good

nor happy

they need to look

into real definitions

of these words

much more clearly/honestly

as they need to

with so many other words

...

otherwise it is just

nonstop grind in hell

all the good people

most people here
are pretty sure
that they are good people
its the rest of the world that is mad & bad

it doesn't add up
a world consisting mainly of good people
cannot be mad & bad
which it clearly is
the only logical conclusion therefore is
that the majority of people are not as good as they think

nothing is more traumatizing to
people than the revelation
that their self is not good
in fact for many it is a ball of negative qualities
they defend and they cry and they scream
some say they are just pawns in an evil system
thats true but why would good
willingly become pawn in an evil system

if only they could
admit gracefully
to the inherent evil within
their road to redemption won't be so tough

network of shared madness

its clear
majority of people on this planet are mad

they are destroying themselves
body, mind & soul
and their environment as well
all at breakneck speed too

there is however a funny system in place
called society
where
all the mad people
agree upon a common definition of sanity
which is simply
being part of the mad system
without questioning

they all think that
they are not mad
as long as a billion other people
think and do as they do
so in this
network of shared madness
no one is allowed to reflect on their own madness
or of the network as a whole
instead the madness passes off as sanity
& anyone pointing out the madness
is in turn labeled mad

busy

from the vantage point of
being part of the very lonely club
of those having oodles of time
it looks like a very busy-busy world
full of watchgazing inhabitants
no-one has any time to even finish a conversation
there is always something important to be done
at first you think that only celebrities have a packed schedule
but then you look at the common people & knock knock
they are all hyperbusy as well
even idle potsmokers are busy smoking pot
with 'do not disturb' signs on their doors
what is surprising is the amount of confidence
people have in their 'doing'
they seem to gno for sure that whatever they
are doing is really important
the multiverse will surely come to a grinding halt
if they through some cruel twist of fate
happen to stop doing their ceaseless 'doing'
everyone is too busy to have any
breathing space to reflect upon
what exactly they are doing

hardly come across anyone who has
any time to spare to interact
one needs appointments for that
kind of stuff to be crammed in
somewhere within their packed itinerary
interaction for evolution
is not even considered

all interaction has to fit within
concrete societal constructs
& evolution is not one of the items on the agenda
its all about business = busy-ness

even those with nothing to do
are busy listening to all the crazy voices
in their head
one way or the other everyone is busy
working for some unknown goal
unknown to me that is
not to them
their short term / long term goals
make complete sense to them
maybe one day they will make sense to me too
till then i will leave them scrubbing their cars / goods
& taking care of their business
while yours truly keeps playing, chatting & smiling from the bed ...

restlessness

majority of people's actions are not guided

by any real purpose or intent

but

by restlessness

if the intent is not to serve the divine

there is an inner lack of bliss & fulfillment

which leads to restlessness

this restlessness is the main driving engine of evil

all that is unnecessary & negative & devoluting

stems from this perpetual neverending restlessness

pointlessness

most of the activities
being done in this world
are pointless

pointless in the sense they are not geared
for evolution
either of the planet or the people

the few sane voices
are getting lost
in the din of the sea of pointlessness

what they who are responsible for this mess
don't realize though is
that the power of divine
is much more
than the power of
the sheer numbers which
make up this jungle of pointlessness

without a connection to P
all is P-oint-less

finding before acting

people
don't seem to be able
to stop
doing/getting entangled in actions
before they have found out
what they are actually supposed to do

they feel compelled by their mind
& society
to just keep doing
& this pointless/directionless doing is
the cause of all problems
on this earth

taking time off
around the age of 16–17
when conscious life is beginning
to sort out
existential dilemmas
seems so hard for them

it is the most natural thing
for a being
to take time to reflect
upon one's existence
& its purpose

it was the first thing

even *brahma* the creator

did

as soon as he came into consciousness

but these days

natural

is hard to find

they have turned against nature

&

have become

un-natural

the lie

people here

start with

a simple lie

that

they gno

what to do here

after

that

its all a lie

taking care of one's own interest

to

take care of

one's own interest

is

a basic urge

in

all beings

and there is nothing wrong with it

no matter how many out there

try to induce guilt trips about it

wrong

only starts

when beings feign

that they

gno

how to

take care of their own interest

without

really gnoing it

...

the Root cause ...

there are too many theories/speculations
about the cause of the
enormous amount of misery on this planet
but they all miss
the root cause

the root cause
of all misery
in this world
is
just one
& its quite simple

the false/fake confidence
that one gnos
what to do
&
how to live
without
really gnoing anything at all
about one's own self
or
this multiverse

the only & the biggest crime
one can commit

a being

who doesn't really gno

and

acts like they gno

what they are doing

can not

escape

hell, pain & torture

it is a straightforward consequence

what happens in movies like 'saw'

& all the goriness & tragedies reported in the media

is just a mild preview

of the future of

such

beings

in divine's eyes

it is the only & biggest crime

anyone can commit

some say

they don't believe in

hell

lotusocean doesn't see

where believing or not-believing

even comes into it

hell is pain & torture

& it is all around

even if one looks with semi-consciousness

I can't be ... It can't be

fact is that

most people

on this planet

are in trapped hellish conditions

but

they can't seem to be able to

perceive their situation as such

as

their ego refuses to admit

that there can be hell

around them

I can't be in hell ... It can't be !

most are unable to look at facts & reality

as they stay rooted in irrational unnatural

egoic paradigm

and

until one admits to being trapped in hell

there is

no question of getting out either

hell without pain & torture ?

there are

too many here

who can dissociate

the term

hell

from

pain & torture

&

thus can be in the

ultra-confident

i will do whatever i feel like

i don't care

mode

or even say

i don't mind hell

these very same people

would be screaming and shouting

like animals in a slaughterhouse

at first signs of pain & torture

admit

most would rather
defend or evade or perish
rather than
admit to their situation

besides the honest dignity
which admitting to one's situation gives
it also opens up
a pathway out of one's situation

the importance of this step
cannot be stressed enough
when
situation of most is simply 'trapped in hell'

TraP

there is nothing

to be said

to

those

who don't get a

trapped feeling

stuck here in this matrix

lotusocean Plog

only applies to

those who

have experienced

this trapped feeling

which is something quite easy to do

when one is in this jail-like world

where even death doesn't necessarily guarantee a way out

that is the reason why

so much lying/hoax is done about space travel and such

because

people should not come to gno

they are trapped inside a jail-world

with a firmament

basically a large petri-dish

for those
who understand and feel the TraP
the opposite
P-ar-T
PT the aR-Ra – NewSun
is the way out

gone to the moon ...

majority of people
here
don't face the fact
on a personal level
that they are stuck here
so it's no wonder then
that lies are rampant
on a collective level
continuous lies like
they have gone to the moon
are going to mars ...
when they don't have a single real proper photograph
(only madeup composites, paintings ...)
of earth to show
from all their purported space travels

planet of the apes ten times over ...

suicide/escape

two major realizations which turn
people towards
suicide (a term for childish escape attempt) –
awareness of being trapped in a hell
awareness of self's imperfections & disabilities

nothing wrong with these conclusions
(parents, psychiatrists and society will tell you otherwise!)
in fact they are necessary for any kind of evolution
its just that
people are not taught simple facts like –
'suicide will not solve the problem
just increase it'

the body can be killed easily
but the 'stupid self' they are running from
will always survive
to face the music
under even more trying circumstances

emergency of emergence

souls/beings here seem to have
no sense of emergency
when it comes to
breaking out of this collapsing matrix
rather than take action immediately
they need to actually think about it
long and hard

when searching for the reason behind this
one comes to realize that
they have other urgent matters to attend to
like paying bills on time
meeting office deadlines
changing oil in the car
sense of emergency is already reserved
for
catching flights & trains
getting to appointments on time
problems with the mobile

emergency = emerging from a contingency
they do act like they have no idea
what the contingency is
so there is no question of emergence

the Boats on an Ocean

other people
might see a
lot happening here
but
what
LotusOcean
sees
is just
beings
each on their own boat
drifting
on an Ocean
trying to find the shore

most don't have a clue
some have some clue
but no one can actually do it
many of the boats
are all battered and leaking water
after
aeons of aimless drifting
many are sinking
but
funnily
no one
asks for direction or helP

...

even those who sometime
come across the
LotusOcean boat
(guaranteed shore access)
and
lower their ego down for a few seconds to ask for help
end up
teaching/preaching
the very next minute

...

all very amusing

...

help ?!

almost all of the effort
in this world
is going into
proving
'we are not in hell'
&
thus don't need help
&
those that don't want help
cannot be hell-ped
out of hell

if one takes 'P' out of help
one is left with hell
quite fitting
since 'P' can help
one out of hell

how helpless get help

helpless

by definition is

a person in a situation

which they are unhappy with

but are unable

to change it

through their own efforts

if one looks at it

with clear perception

this state applies to

majority of the people

on this planet

the strange bit is

only few are able to

admit to it

& only these few

who ask for help

get a helping hand by divine

out of their unwanted state

no one in denial

can ever be helped

when they say
'god helps those
who help themselves'
they forgot to explain
what helping oneself is

helping oneself is
being honest about one's state
and one's inability to change it through
one's own efforts
helping oneself is actually
asking/praying to
divine for help
in a humble manner

death and life

those who

do not

face the

reality

of

death

and

learn how

to die successfully

cannot

really

live

either

.

billionaires

people
want to be
billionaires
in some way
and since most
cant be that with money
they act it out
with time

everyone is a
billionaire
when it comes to time
when the actual
account balance is
usually max
100 years

thats why
they act very surprised
when time is about to be up
oh wait
i thought i had billions left still
they say

the reason why

the reason why
majority of people on this planet
live their life like they do
is
because they assume/presume
that it will all last forever
their parents, friends, pets
and of course them

in this foreverness
one can while away time
doing
one silly frivolosity/triviality
after another
whats the harm they say
we have all the time in the world
an eternity for nonsense

looking at them
one gets the feeling
they have infinite lifespans
beings here show no
comprehension
of their lifespan

reality of death
does not ever really
enter their
consciousness

when it actually happens
in their forever-little-world
it is seen as a trauma
which they usually cannot recover from

death opens up too many questions
like what after etc
so best to just behave
as if it doesn't exist
& carry on with mindless
nonsense in
foreverland

a being who gnos
that they have limited time here
is bound to behave differently
especially if they also gno
what is at stake
if they don't

there are too many here

who think

that

if they dont

think

about the future

(ignore it completely)

and keep on living

just reacting to

the momentary happenings

within their narrow confines

it (future) will never come

i.e

it will never become the present

thus so much head-in-the-sandness

about

realities like death, afterlife etc

next half an hour

there are too many here
who believe in doing actions
without even
considering/visualizing the
future of
next half an hour
let alone
'til death
or after death
or
the many cycles of birth & death

&

all of them
can't seem to figure
out why
things go so wrong for them

hmmm

a refusal

most

people

refuse to consider

the future

short term or long term or full term

but

future always

still

arrives

&

becomes the

PresenT

always

an unpleasant present

when one has

not had any

consideration

for it

consideration

consideration
a term now relegated
to how one is with others

lotusocean says
consideration
is
a term
which has to be
applied
first to one's own self

considering
one's own
whole full future
(incl death & cycle of birth & death)
fully
being the
only
way
to
get out of all hell & unpleasantness

CONSIDER

CONSIDER

the most important

word

required for the

people on this planet

it should

(in bold letters)

replace

all signs, boards, grafitti, ads

everywhere

should be

C for CONSIDER in all schoolbooks

coz

refusal to

CONSIDER

fully, properly, completely

before

acting

is

the source

of all ills

which plague them

CONSIDER

='s

Concentric Sides

i.e

looking at

things from all sides

& angles

before

taking any

Decision

CONSIDER is a full circle

in itself

nothing left out

especially the core issue at hand

to CONSIDER

is an automatic natural thing

its about facts

not just thinking & lies of ego

if one is over-riding it

for whatever reason

one should gno

it will always lead to

hell, pain & torture

NO

the second most

important

word

for the people of this planet

after one

CONSIDERS

it is an

automatic

NO

to

all

Nonsense

the only

way

out of

the

hellish matrix

only after

NO

to the rest

can one say

YES

to

DIVINE

CONCERN

a

sister word for

CONSIDER

and

both

are related to that

most enormous thing

in the multiverse

FUTURE

without

CARE

CONCERN

&

CONSIDERATION

for

totality of

one's

FUTURE

one

cannot

have

a

good

FUTURE

&

if you can do any math

you will gno

FUTURE

is a long long long long long

billion trillion ad infinitum ...

time

to be in

boredom, hell, pain & torture

elePhant in the room

there is only one
elePhant in the room
for anyone anywhere
&
that elePhant
is their
Future (Phuture)
this life, death & afterlife and so forth
much bigger than the past they can remember
or the fleeting present
the hugest biggest thing
which
everyone ignores
like
it
doesn't exist

if one
refuses to acknowledge
there is a thing
called
the future
(in fact show a finger to it
when it enters one's consciousness
like most are doing)
the future
cannot be good

no surprises there

when
future sticks the finger back to them
the whole bravado vanishes quite quickly

FUTURE

Future
is
Phuture
P-hu-tur-e
P-who-turns-energyspirals
so
basically
P
the Axis
is
Phuture

if one has no
concern for future
one
will have no
hesitation in
ignoring
P

how many in this world
are really concerned
for their Phuture
is
seen easily in this light
:)

nothing to be said

there is
nothing to be said
to beings
who
don't
care about
the phuture
of their
own
self/being

the only voice
they will get to hear
is that of the
consequences

a state of constant surprise

there are too many here
that think
they are some invincible supreme being
who will face
no consequence
for their actions

funnily
when the consequences arrive
like the vomiting & nausea
after boozing
they are well surprised

they are surprised
each & every time
any consequence comes back at them
for their
actions (which are of course done without any real gnoing)

sums up the whole muggle-world kindergarten society out there
a constant state of surprise
& bewilderment
how did things go so bad suddenly?

consequences

most people

do what they do

only

because

they simply do not gno

the consequences of what they do

if they did gno

the concentric sequences

that follow

most would not do the deeds they do

thats why

gnowledge

of

consequences

is the

real gnowledge

the real seeing

of

seers

principal operating system

'life is but a joke'

is the

principal operating system

of most

on this planet

of course

some beings

stick to their principle

more than others

thus only

some are on the frontline

whether on the frontline or backline

there has to be a conscious decision

to fully uninstall

the prinicipal operating system

and

properly

install

a new futurecentric one

'life is serious business with serious consequences'

the fact

people

have a habit

of projecting their

notions and part-gnowledge

as

facts

but

in reality

they don't gno a

single fact

worth gnoing

a real fact

is one

which helps

get one out of hell

and

break out of the 3-d matrix

if only

they could admit

they don't really gno any fact

they could at least begin

on the PaTh of learning

facts

stairway to heaven

only
real
stairway to heaven
is
the
stairway of facts

sticking to facts

with facts
just perceiving them
is not
good enough
sticking to them
in speech and action
is
much more important

facts

facts
real spelling
Ph-acts

so acts
done as per
P
the
Axis
that sees
it all
for
what
it is

the one & only disease

on the surface
there appear to be many diseases
plaguing beings on this planet
lotusocean however sees
only one disease
which is
not being able to state the obvious truth

people lie to each other
about each other's state
every day trillions of times
straightforward speaking out of obvious perception
is looked down upon like a cardinal sin
petty egos have to be saved blushes
at all costs

this vow of never speaking out of truth
leads to a real dis - ease
within the self
& then the world

if people just practiced
speaking what is as is
without crazy agendas
all diseases are sure to disappear

evil was only born
from not wanting to speak of
the obvious divinity of divine

Praise Phacts

Acknowledging
Phacts (asa Facts)
Speaking
Phacts
Reiterating
Phacts
is
what
automatically
leads to
Praise
of
Higher
&
Divine

so if
one
can't
simply
roll along with
Phact Phlow
one
can't
Praise
either
and
one
will
devolve

...

mute idols & living god

after playing

around with

mute idols

for

millennia

the masses

are not ready for a living god

they would rather

have a mum empty idol

who doesn't answer back

who they can treat in any which way

put in any kind of dingy cage

throw any kind of stuff at

ask any kind of unwholesome favours

a living god

is a passionate force

too hot for them to handle

in their insincere ways

god & pain

one of the biggest misconceptions =
'god is in everyone/where/thing'

how 'god' is not in 'everything'
can be understood in many ways

there is a scientific way,
a psychological way
& a consciousness way

these ways are all ultimately connected

the best & most simplest way however
is to understand it in terms of
'pain' and 'painlessness'

for example – 'god' doesn't exist in 'playstation'
which at the end of the day
lowers consciousness and brings pain to the
players in terms of physical & astral

you see 'god' is not into 'pain' &
'godlyness' is 'a state of conscious painlessness'

realms of pain, torture & karmic bondage
having nothing to do with god
the real god never intended creation to be like that

ultimately, all IS one, yes? you ask

i say 'No'

these kinds of assumptions only suit the
evil demiurge's plan at the end of the day

people think that 'all is one' and consequently
they are accepting of everyone as they are,
which in the end plays straight into the hands
of the manipulators

they want 'you' to accept 'them'
and in doing so suffer at their hands

for example a female with this mindset & logic
will go ahead and sleep with any male
(because after all 'all is one' and whats the harm)
as a result her vibrations go down further
and the spiderwebs tighten
this attitude doesn't allow
one to break from this matrix of pain

'all is connected' is a more apt statement than
'all is one'
a good education tool
to teach people the effects of actions

the multiverses emanated from 'the one'
in time the energies of certain levels
of this multiverse were manipulated
to create something 'ungodly' i.e 'pained'
it became 'painful – full of pain' in course of time

and in these ungodly 'realms' more and more
artificial stuff keeps on getting created –
bionic robots, clones, soulless androids
etc etc.

there exist realms which have no pain –
emotional, psychological or physical

there everything is 'godly'
because they maintain connection with
'the divine one' at all points

the beings which deliberately sever
that connection create ungodly realms
which are not part of 'the one'
simply because they don't adhere to
'the one's' specifications for creation

such creations obviously involve a whole lot
of pain & torture & work on maxims like
'no pain no gain'

so you can understand 'godliness'
as a kind of way; not a thing or substance
most of this 3-D physical realm on
this planet is not functioning by that way
and thus is not godly

what physical & psychological pain is
can be understood scientifically and
thats where true sciences like
sacred geometry come in

so yes 'everything is not god'
there is 'a moving away from god'
and thats why there is 'pain'

the santa claus notion

there are many here who
think/feel that
GoD is a being
whose sole purpose is
to fulfill their desires
no matter how bad/infringing those wantings are
for other beings or nature
that they are against
divine laws
should not matter either
their wants & likes are primary
rest is secondary
including GoD

GoD as a playful observer
who always sides with those
who exist in accordance with divine laws
doesn't sit well with their
GoD as santa claus bearing candies
notions

they say thats why many people
don't believe in GoD anymore
because it doesn't cater
to their crazy unwholesome whims and fancies
like the evil system does

its surprising though
that they are still not happy
in the evil system
suicidal or close to it in most cases
as they continue their tirade against GoD

GoD's (mis)image

in the so-called west
if it (GoD) is not a
sullen looking being with a
crown of thorns
it is a dreary looking old uncle
with santa-like white beard
spewing boring dialogues

basically anything which
females can not feel attraction towards

if females get disassociated with god
society automatically will

a very fine way of reducing
interest in god
make it seem boring
as compared to evil

a god that is
youthful
sexy
blissful
interesting beyond imagination
intelligent
playful
fun
rocking

would completely
upturn the whole edifice
their hellish world stands on

vedic conception of god
was always embodied by the 'krishn' archetype
the alluring enchanter
the lover
the P-layer
because thats what God (divine) is
a role which evil has been trying to
play ...

unsuccessfully

gods of their liking

in bharat the land of deities
no matter where one looks
one finds pictorial representations
of the 'trinity' especially
shiv & vishnu
thats not a bad thing in itself
but for the fact that
they all look like fat shopkeepers

talk about making god in your image
or your desired state's image
or simply your liking & convenience

in the last 100 years one can
see these representations
change
from leaner to fatter

not surprising in a decaying culture
which sees chubbiness
as a sign of prosperity
and fattyness as the emblem of 'personality'

the female deities
are all based on faces/physiques
of popular bollywood actresses

even the representations from the west
convey more deitylike qualities
simply bcoz they don't suffer
from the worship of plump bollywood stars

if this is what is being worshipped
one is not surprised by the results

pictorial human representation of deities
belonging to other dimensions
is a subtle tricky process
requiring coming together of the
best of everything
not a pandering to the
convoluted programmed aspirations of the
lowest common denominator

the judges of greatness

there is
general (mis)conception
amongst the masses of this planet
that a being is only great
if it does not reveal its own qualities
instead allowing
others to reveal its qualities

this would make
krishn
an incarnation of divine
not a great being
as he revealed
his own qualities
from his own mouth
in a talk now called 'bhagawadgita'

the masses think
they are qualified
to judge qualities of
a soul
which is much higher than them in
evolutionary status

it is an
illogical impossibility
they can never come to gno the
partial attributes
let alone complete attributes
of a being
way beyond themselves

their conception of great
only stretches to what they can perceive
so what they call great
is someone basically

at the same level as themselves
in other words
they are great

would be laughable
if not so
detrimental to their evolution

greater than *god*

its funny how most people expect *the source*, *the most high*
to fit their own parameters
so if *the source* manifests itself into this world
& its parameters fall outside of their assigned parameters
then it surely cannot be *god*
most people despite not being absolute experts
in any field are absolute experts when it comes to
one subject – *god*
everyone seems to gno what *god* would be/should be like
if it were to manifest
especially how it will treat them i.e
accept them as they are
while they judge & ridicule it
those who conclude *god* doesn't exist at all
also have to be geniuses
considering the all-gnoing nature of this conclusion
so its settled
'all the people' are greater than *god*
because they have parameters outside of *god*
while *god* only has parameters assigned by them
makes one roll on the ground with laughter

we can tell 'god' when we see it

its funny
how beings here
hope to be able to recognize
'the one, the avatar, the saviour'
using their own
faulty perceptions

most of them cannot even fathom
who is truly higher than them
let alone fathom the highest

they find
the media-made celebrities to be higher
when they are just as lowly as them
maybe lower even
while some unpretentious villager
in a real culture
they would define as lower

one needs to have honesty
& humility to the divine
to be able to see
the beauty & marks of divinity
& the humility has to be strong enough
to overcome feelings like jealousy & self-loathing
when one has seen it

temples

all the temples
of every organized
religion
on this planet
are a fraud
they serve the
fat priests
not
divine

the only real temple
is the
temple area
of the avatar's head

(w)holy

the term 'holy'
comes from
'wholly'
'w' is silent as always

to be whole
is the only way
to be holy

(w)holywood not hollywood –
youtu.be/zIpb9Kdy9qc

religion

when god/divine appears
in flesh & blood
in front of a person
and
they just run towards a structure called temple
then they are a hindu
if they run towards a structure called a mosque
then they are a muslim
if they run towards a structure called a church
then they are a christian
etc etc etc

religion was about
re linking (re-li-gion) with god
now it is just linking with
unfractal structures of their own making
which have nothing to do with
god/divine

even the sanctity of these
unfractally built and maintained structures
is always being compromised

a really insincere state of affairs

there is no such thing as Yoga

breaking news –
there is no such thing as Yoga

this term Yoga has now
become synonymous with
contorting of the body into various shapes
but the truth is that
there is no such word

the real word in Sanskrit is 'Yog'
just like Shiva is actually 'Shiv'
Krishna is actually 'Krishn'
Veda is actually 'Ved'
& so forth

'Yog' simply means 'Union'
'Union with the Divine'
to be precise

this Union takes place through
devotion, surrender, praise & service
to the high & divine

it has nothing to do with the asans
commonly gnown as asanas
being taught in the west
Yoga Classes which are now
hard to tell apart from Aerobics Oz Style
act mainly as respectable health & dating centers
males flock to see females in postures
they won't see them in otherwise
no wonder Yoga has caught on
like it has
to turn into a
global corporate entity with
Yoga drinks, gear, clothing etc etc
so its either Yoga or Yog
another 21st century choice ...

how to tell between
fake & real gurus

many in this world
are duped by charlatans
because they don't seem to be aware
of the
distinguishing
marks/traits/signs of the higher/more divine

society has only one definition for holy
'no sex or sexuality/beauty '
all any ugly charlatan has to do is put on a celibate image
to get adoration
however in this age of cameras they often get caught
everyone gets disappointed &
starts losing all faith in holyness/divine

to clear this up
lotusocean states that
the more enlightened/higher/divine can always be
distinguished
not by their lack of sexuality or age
but
by their connection to elements/nature

for example
if a musician plays for rain
& rain happens
that musician is a more evolved soul
& thus closer to divine

nature not only follows the will of divinity
but plays with it

in this 3-d world
the higher/divine is easy to spot
through
their superior more graceful
sound & light
(voice, music, image, movement)

most can see it
even though many might not like to admit to it
through negative feelings like jealousy

also
the enlightened will always speak
clear precise truth

without any fear of the repercussions
unlike charlatans
who speak to please
who say mumbo jumbo which doesn't make any sense
& spins people around in circles

the truth is that these fake gurus don't gno the truth
they don't even gno about the truth of this world
let alone other worlds

the enlightened don't wear fake smiles
like the fake gurus of today
who resemble newsreaders
in putting on cringy fake smiles

the happiness of the higher/divine is real
& comes from real gnoing of their own divinity
& the ability to navigate their soul after death

& while here they live fractal lives
i.e everything falls into place perfectly
in whatever they do

COW

those who
cannot respect the cow
whose milk they drink
cannot respect
earth which is akin to a cow
in fulfilling our needs
no question of
them respecting
god/divine either

people hoping to
find
love, peace, happiness
contentment & evolution
while killing & eating cows
are under
serious delusion

in the end
they would
meet a cruel fate
at the hands
of
forces of divine

(w) holy cow

"holy cow"
a widely used expression
unfortunately
not put in practice
by majority of this planet

there is no doubt that
cow is the supreme
amongst all the animals that
roam this earth
it is earth itself in a more compact lovable form
the fact that majority of people
drink its milk makes it a real mother to all

still how this mother is treated
by a vast majority of this planet
except parts of Bharat (now called india)
determines
the hellish state
those parts of the world have to endure

the blissless pain & torture twilight zone
which they are under
is a direct result of this mistreatment

until
they start treating cows right
they will have all the diseases, wars
mental hells, blisslessness ...

what they do to the cows
they will face back manifold
in this life & afterlife

this simple truth
& simple action
can solve 99% of this worlds problems
& humanify the not so human population here

2 Cow-Ways

there are 2 kinds of
ways of keeping cows

in one
you let them
graze freely
they always come back to you
because they have a proper bond with you
you only take as much milk as
they freely want to give you
after feeding their calves
you milk them by hand
you keep them till their dying day

in the other
you keep them within fences
as they would never come back
if you let them go
put crazy stuff in their food
to make them give more milk
squeeze as much milk as you can
through machines
kill them when they stop giving milk

no point pointing out
which way is better

the difference between these 2 ways
is difference between
human & barbarian/demonic

not all-right when not right-at-all

there is a constant
almost lunatic
repetition of
'its alright'
'its going to be alright'
in the so-called west

its a pathetic impractical joke
they play on themselves
coz
nothing is ever going to be all-right
in their hell-bound not-right way
not
until the way is changed completely
&
cows are treated right
those who mistreat/kill cows
find hell in this life
&
experience it in their afterlife too
there is no doubt in that fact

cow is the very representation of earth
its the mother principle on this plane
those who unleash violence against the cow
have no right to & will not last on this earth

what goes in

those
who cannot even
take responsibility
for
what goes into
their mouth
cannot be expected
to take responsibility
for anything else
including their
soul

they can't be bothered about
how the animal was killed
who killed it
how was it kept
what was it fed
what is their relation to it
all they care about
is the meat on the plate
which they can gobble up
mindlessly
& use that
negative tamasic cursed energy
for mindless pointless pursuits

and what to say
of those
who praise these
actions & pursuits

meat & violence

in the so-called west
they have gone to great lengths
to disconnect themselves from
what they eat
so if its 'beef' one is eating
it has nothing to do with a cow
when one is eating 'pork'
its nothing to do with a pig
when one is eating 'mutton'
its nothing to do with sheep
& so on and so forth

there is not much wanting to gno
how that stuff got to their table either
its uncivilized to even mention
the violence involved
just close your senses/mind/heart
& chew

talk about head in the sand
in a wonky witches tale
funny how the very same people
talk about
love, freedom & justice ...

the meat consciousness
based on unnecessary violence towards animals
which is prevalent on this planet
makes it impossible for
there to be any real positive change

most cannot even fathom that
violence amongst people
cannot be stopped
unless violence towards fellow creatures
is stopped

as long as there are cages for
chickens & cows
there will be cages for
homo erectus too
the way they cut them down
the same way they will be cut down too

the meatspell

there are forces
which are making
meat easily available
in huge amounts in big stores
beings all over this planet
are falling for it
pigging out
and turning into
pigs and beasts

never has so much meat
been available
even all hunter-tribes
only ate to survive
when you have to kill to eat
gluttony is not easy to come by

they haven't been told
the price they will pay for it
let them be informed that
it would be way-beyond their
debit & credit cards

it's common gnowledge what
pigs are fattened for

cruel unnecessary
spirit-sapping dependency

when people get to hear about
facts like
many of the pills
they buy at pharmacies
including anti-depressants, viagra etc
are made from bodies of homo sapiens
they get panicky

they think hannibal/cannibal is only reserved for movies

they don't see
how easily this kind of dependency comes about
when a certain path is taken
nowadays it's easy for many people
to get to a state
where they say
they can't have a meal without chicken
and then soon it is
they cannot eat a meal without cow's meat
so where is the line drawn
which will stop them from feeling the same way
about homo-sapiens & their organs

so those who have gone down this path
have become the real rakshasas now
vampires are not just in movies
they are a reality

a straightforward result
of
turning against divine

torture removal

most people
on this planet
are torturing their
own bodies
or
the bodies of others
mostly they are doing both
most don't even realize
they are doing it

this is done under various
guises
from duty to love to spirituality

the fact is
nothing real
like
true bliss or happiness or evolution
can ever be achieved
through torture

divine is comfort oriented
not torture oriented
only evil creates
false notions like
'no pain no gain'
the truth is
'no gain through pain'
only gain comes through
praise of divine
and that doesn't require any pain or torture

unconscious zombies

this world is
full of
unconscious zombies
who keep on
screaming
'ouch'
after they hit
stones and walls
continuously
in their unrestrained
unconsciousness

put their
hand in fire
time after time
and forget that
it burns
from the last time

to get conscious
is a choice
&
not many seem interested
as they have
no shame
about being unconscious

automatic consciousness ?

people here strive for a lot of things
but they take
consciousness for granted
as if anything
which is born
will automatically have
consciousness

consciousness
is not an automatic thing
it is something
which one has to strive for
continuously
because if one lets up even for a second
one loses it

the art of deliberate ignoring

the genesnakes
haven't learnt much in their
long crawl out here
but
they all seem to have learnt
the noble art of deliberate ignoring
some are more expert at it than others

it goes like this –
whenever they see some being
more interesting & attractive than themselves &
thus naturally feel drawn towards it
they immediately retract
& feign that they are not interested at all
instead they try to attract the other being
in their limited ways
males usually jump around crazily
showing off their physical prowess
females jot out their mammary glands and
change their gait
couples start snogging each other
after making sure they are in line of sight
some try & show off their
skills/gnowledge in loud conversations
some just pretend to be overtly happy & satisfied
some start staring into their mobile
with unflinching penance-like concentration
some go to crazy lengths to appear busy
nothing subtle about this art

what they hope to gain
from this strategy
besides giving the higher being some laughs
is hard to conceive
after all
who needs who

boring & interesting

fact – many are bored, really bored
so bored that the safety mindlessly associated with boring
has gotten boring too
mindlessly i say coz boring = safe means dumb = safe
dumbness leads to accidents / disasters not safety
so why do they cling to the dumb & boring
& not make a movement
towards the more intelligent & interesting ?
interesting not in the sense of
'bungee jumping' coz that gets boring too
after one or 2 tries

interesting in terms of the
'real gnowledge of all aspects of multiversal existence'
i.e really interesting

in this hyper-connected world
where more interesting can always be found
there are no excuses
but still very few actually are able to do it
maybe this scenario will help explain

people on buses, trains, airports hide their faces
in books that lead nowhere
& pretend that they never saw you
they would 'be' the same even if 'god' walked by
a difficult to pull-off-act considering the
huge gulf between interesting & boring
at play in the situation
but they achieve the impossible
by robotically repeating this holy chant loudly in their head –
book is more important
book is more important
i have chosen the book
my choice is no.1 priority
i am in control of the book
through the book i am in control of the situation

replace book with pet, partner, mobile & so forth
& you get the picture

the Biggest Addiction ~ only Real Epidemic

contrary to

the general belief

its not

alcohol

or

drugs

most

beings

here

are

addicted

to

getting attention

from others

(for no apparent rhyme or reason)

is the

biggest

addiction

out here

it takes them all

straight to hell

...

giving attention to

higher & divine

&

Praise with Proper diction

is the only

cure

for

this

massive

addiction

jumpin' & yellin'

lots of

beastly and bratty

jumping and yelling

going on by the various genesnakes

here

to get attention

some more than others

they call it music, sports etc etc

what they would actually

do with each other's attention

remains a mystery

the MAS in MASSES

deep down

everyone at some point or other

feels small

but when one is actually confronted

with something higher

treating one as one ought to be treated

one's reaction is that of unease

through the peculiar functionings of the ego

one knows one is small

but in society one is always used

to being treated like one isn't

there is a whole net of mutual assurance

in place

to keep the ego afloat

thus the term

MAS: Mutual Assurance Society

no real-evolution is possible without the

ego cracking

something which is a taboo in this

'celebration of the self' world

buildings

what do people really
believe in these days ?
'buildings'
is the simple answer
in buildings we trust
not god or divine
just
concrete, glass and metal
ugly & unbreathable
thats why they happily
send their kids to so-called universities
which is nothing but a bunch of buildings
what do buildings have to do with
imparting any real gnowledge

they are just impressed by buildings
banks, towers, malls, courts, 5 star hotels
they are the symbol for all that is right
& all that is good
buildings which actually
negatively affect
the human biology
& soul

they gravitate to buildings
like moths to a flame

the flames of hell
in this case

they think these buildings
will last forever
& save them from
wrath of the higher forces
all the evidence points
to the contrary
time will tell

heaven

what can be said of
a planet
where the major faction
of the population's
idea of
heaven
is
shopping malls

concrete structures
full of useless things
airconditioning &
bright lights
which can ruffle
any electro-biological functioning
in other words
something really bad
for human body & soul

heaven
used to be the
name for
self-sustaining em field
which was entered through
a fractal life &
a successful death
where angels stayed
the angels
being the elements

hospital

hospital
a good place in
the mind of the masses
of this planet
whosoever is getting them built
is considered a good person

just some children seem to be afraid of it
for good reasons too
what it really is is
a cold concrete unfractal hellhole
lit up by mindnumbing tubelights
made to suck life out of
any biological entity
it is a place
where they administer poisons
& do butchery

its better to die in
an open field
than die in a hospital

its the very opposite of
a place of healing
which is always
made up of natural materials
and
all cures are natural as well

material science

out of sheer ignorance
as to what
certain metals/alloys,
concrete and other
synthetic materials do to
one's body & aura
people of this planet
keep on building
edgy ugly structures
with these unfractal unembeddable materials
everywhere

its not just ugly
to the eye
to behold a
tinroofed concrete structure in the
middle of a pristine nature spot
it actually disrupts the
electromagnetics of the whole area
stuff which eyes cannot see
but can actually be measured

it is poisonous
in the same way
artificial chemicals in food
are poisonous
only in this case
the results are seen/felt over time
and the cause remains unknown
next time you have a migraine in
your cramped concrete metro flat
please don't look around for reasons
where they don't exist
or listen to your doctor
just try fresh air in a forest area

science has now reached the point
where it can
scientifically prove that this is the case
but this information is not made
available to the public
for the sake of protecting the
interests of the construction companies
& all the associated businesses
in much the same way as truth about
pills/drugs they sell at your local pharmacist
is not revealed
in order to keep pharmaceutical companies in play

there is still some awareness about pills etc
amongst masses
but material science
is completely out of the awareness-zone of
the average person on the street

the net result is the same
the population of this planet poisons itself
and its environment

the rulers of this psychosystem
do not care
the blissless depraved beings they are
just coz they know they are going down
in their rebellion with divine
they just want to take as many down with them

151

5 star hotels

while the
majority of this earth's population
faces the hell of
malnutrition & unhy(high)genic living conditions

the so-called lucky people
with the funny quantity called money
face the hell that is
5 star hotel
the final shangrila of this system

the 5 stars stand for
dingy, concretey, claustrophobic, unbreathable & unfractal
any real being with properly functioning
nerves & biological processes
can get headache/dizziness within half an hour
the food served there takes the
digestive system on a rollercoaster ride
while the airconditioning
works on giving the guest a cold
all in all
a much more dangerous place for biological entities
than any slum in an open field

whole lotta rubbish

no matter where you go
on this planet
you will encounter rubbish

in the so-called developed countries
it is sort of hidden in stockpiles
called landfills
some of which are the size of small countries
in the so-called developing countries
it is strewn all over everywhere
you cannot miss it no matter
how hard you try

all sacred places have it
all lovely nature places have it
there is some local variation
beer bottles in west
gutka packets in east

development ='s rubbish generation
more development means more rubbish
most of it non-biodegradable

all this waste for nothing
are people happier ?
no

wasteful actions
of a wasteful people
only rubbish spewing from their
mouth, thoughts & actions

they talk about
whole lotta love
but the fact is just
whole lotta rubbish
it seems their love just
produces rubbish
its definition definitely
needs looking into

wash-mania

there is a whole lot of washing
going on in this world
people repeatedly rubbing & scrubbing
themselves, their cars & their homes

the waters around the world get polluted
but the filth never goes away

after a zillion baths
they still do not realize
that only real filth is within

the enemy is not the dust
but the internal attitude
which is mis-aligned with the divine
& that won't go away by
any amount of washing powders

rice naturally propagated by
gobar (cowdung)

culture and agri-culture

the so-called west

which is basically just a term for
translucent occupied territory

did not have any

culture

so it is pointless to expect them to have

agri-culture

they did a really bad job of learning it too

&

the worst part

they have been / are spreading

their own

hellish mechanical chemical genetically modified anti life version

all over the planet

&

even worse part is that

others have adopted this madness

myth of independence

the word 'independence'
stands out
amongst the many buzzwords
of the 20th century (from an arbitrary reset)
lots of violence has been unleashed
for the sake of this word

many proudly
proclaim themselves as
'independent'
just because they are
able to support themselves financially
through one means or the other

so is financial independence
independence?
what about all the prisons in
the mind?
and is there any real financial
independence? the day the banks say
this credit/account is not valid
one loses their fictional financial independence

same goes for the handdrawn lines called countries
there have been major wars of independence
in america, india & the rest
but who got independent & from whom?
to my eyes its still a
'United Kingdom'

all the so called independent countries
are all in debt to a mysterious organization called
'world bank' &
all are dependent on it for loans
to keep their pseudo-economies going

so when all the so-called countries
got their so-called independence
it was only a sham as the strings
were now going to be pulled through
a more intangible control tool – money
military control took too much effort
financial control was far easier

nobody questioned anything
because they were 'independent'
on a personal level this makes
any person feel good
the ego is satisfied by the
'myth of independence'
when the reality is that
most are just pawns in a game

the definition of independence
has never been asked for
oxford websters dictionary
is satisfactory enough for most
is a person in a prison with metal bars
not independent?

they can think what they like,
dream what they like,
put their attention where they want to.
the only real independence anyone
ever had was to put their attention
where they wanted to i.e
the devil or the divine
this independence is called 'freewill'
and cannot be taken away
by any outside entity or force
unless one misuses it to an extent
that amidst the twists & tangles
one feels
one doesn't have a choice anymore

any other 'independence'
which is sold in this world
is a soap bubble which
as we all gno is not something which lasts too long
all these independences do is
create an unhumble attitude
coz after all even the
Jedis are dependent on *the Force*

land

one doesn't own land

by putting a house on it

by buying it

by inheriting it or

by moving/killing off its rightful owner

one owns land by properly embedding in/with it

even then it is still

on lease from the divine

country of no land

everywhere one hears
'i love my country'
what it means is
i will shamelessly
desecrate and pollute
its land, air & water

surely
country
like corporations
is not a concept
connected to
land, earth, air & water anymore

sheer madness

leaders or misleaders ?!

there are no
leaders
on this planet
only
misleaders

some do it
out of sheer ignorance
some out of sheer evil

the result –
enmasse devolution of souls
great stress on bhoodevi

to lead
one needs
to gno
where one is going first

a notice

beings cannot be

stopped from

ruining themselves

that's their use of freewill

but

they

can't be

won't be

allowed to

ruin the earth

...

for the hell of it

what can be done
for the beings
who have created a hell on this
beautiful earth
and call that hell beautiful

they show no desire to get out of it
no matter how diseased they get
or how polluted everything else gets

this is unprecedented in the history
of this multiverse
this kind of situation has never arisen before
where beings want pain & torture for the
hell of it
no gain coming of it
for body, mind or soul

of course
they would have to be stopped before
they destroy the planet completely
they surely won't mind
being quarantined into some concrete hells
where they won't mind spending
this & the rest of their lives

only 2 kinds

despite all the
race & creeds
on show here
the fact is that
there are only
2 kinds of beings here

one who are ready
to live in harmony with
earth & divine
and care about their
soul evolution

the other are those who
don't mind creating a hell here
& going to one afterwards
they are ready to lose their soul
for sake of ignorance
& anti-divine stances

only one kind
will inherit the earth
the kind kind

the real President

with their limited/twisted perceptions
& disconnected from nature sensibilities
they (the people of this planet) can elect
who they want
as their P-resident or Prime Resident
of their arbitrarily cut pieces of land called countries

but the real President of the whole earth
who can set real Precedents
would always be
what the wind & sea & rain & trees & the elementals
& the earth & the sun & the stars & the universe
& the multiverse elects

this election is based upon
the divinity/fractality within
no rigging possible
as the results are impossible to fake
it follows multiversal natural laws
not contrived absurd structures of society/government
or whims and fancies of mindprogrammed mass zombies

if the people of this planet
choose to
ignore or not-align with this real President
they can forget about peace, happiness
& prepare for ...

the only peaceful solution

peace amongst beings
can only happen
if they are all striving for evolution

otherwise no amount of effort
can bring about that Peace

if they all strive for evolution
their attention would be on
high & divine
not on each other's nonsense

they would also automatically
gno the right behaviour
for any situation
from this attention on divine

peace comes from creating connection to divine
not entangling strings with each other

science to scientism

science

on this planet

has been reduced to

just another religion (scientism)

by its governing institutions (fraudstitutions more-like)

everything they have shoved down

people's throat

in last 500 years

including –

who people are

what earth is

where it is

what universe is

what space is

what phorce is

what sun is

what stars are ...

is all based on

faith/make-believe/we-say-so/bogus-maths

rather than any

reality/observation/proof/logic

&

ALL of it is of course FALSE
because the agenda is to keep people from asking
real questions
rather than answering their questions
and
in an ego-driven populace
which likes to go around like gno-ers
without gno-ing anything firsthand
it's quite easy to
create/maintain a paradigm of LIES
and call it
science

it's worse than the
'planet of the apes' scenario

only now a few are waking up
because of the
Presence of you-gno-who ...

multidimensionality

all the energy
of the
people ruling over all the other people
on this planet
for the last 100 years
has gone into
stopping
dimensional consciousness
from seeping into the
mass consciousness

dimensional consciousness
meaning
there are other
dimensions beyond the 3-d
simple facts like
multiverse
is
multidimensional

everything in education, media etc
is concentrated
on keeping everyone
fully concentrated only on 3-d
false science, sitcoms, movies, sports, aliens ...

they are very worried about
who will slave away for them
if people started focusing on
ways out of the cage
which at the moment they are told
is the only thing that exists
so everyone is just scampering for
whatever little crap they can
find within the cage
instead of
concentrating on
breaking out of it

its all too much ...

it is too much

for most people/sheeple

aka

muggles

to stomach

that ALL they have been told/taught

at/by school/universities/media

is a BIG LIE

& why

is it all too much

because

they have never been honest with themselves

they would rather

keep up their egoic pretense of

false gnoing

& bury their heads in the sand

than face the truth

the

truth

which

can save them from

constant hell

they are in

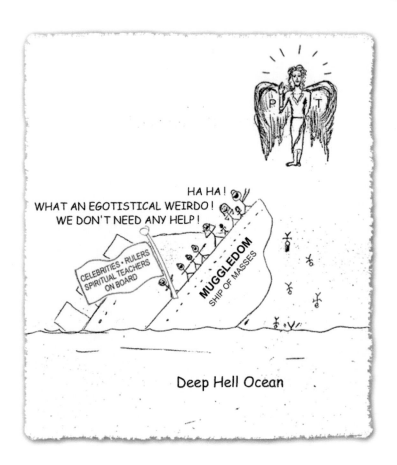

tragicomic

despite all their heavy handed splashing efforts
most beings here
are drowning quickly in the
ocean of this *samsar* (world)
amongst the gasps
as they look up to see that
which is effortlessly standing above it all
they only choose to hurl abuses at it
and scream
'we are in this only by choice
and can get out any time we want
we don't need you or your help'
quite a spectacle
a show of supreme confidence
in the most calamitous of situations

beds & sofas

funny as it might seem
beds & sofas are a big stumbling block
when it comes to developing humility
towards the divine
on this material plane of existence

beds and sofas were delivered at everyones doorstep
through the evil machine massproduction processes
so everyone had a chance to boost their ego
in their own little kingdom
they called home

so whatever skills even the
working, business & military classes
(the ruling class were direct pawns of evil anyways)
had at practical humility
disappeared like clouds on a sunny day

plonked on their sofas
they feel like lords
and find it harder & harder to get up
for any representative of divinity

to hell with divinity when
i am having a good time with my beer
in my sofa
they say

they only get up
for their bosses i.e the representatives of evil
and that too is more
out of a pre-empted kick on the backside

all part of a brat creation policy
of the evil demiurge
physical force & financial pressure
being the only languages
these spoiled brats understand

at the end of the day
who can be taught anything
when he/she is sitting on a sofa
or lying in a bed ...

brat

brat
b-rat
bound rat

bound rats
thats what
majority of
the population here is

and
its not by force
its by
choice

they choose to be
bratty
and
keep on
suffering

...

jobs

job
the most important buzzword in this world
millions of jobs
are being created out of thin air everyday
to keep the dream of
millions alive
dreams of a mobile phone
etc etc

no one has any clue as to what
all these jobs accomplish
at the end of the day
besides being
destructive to earth
& its environment
directly or indirectly

creation of a machine borg world
perhaps

where is this progress
they talk about ?
all there is is just
ugliness (powerlines, concrete hells)
and pollution
more people are starving than ever before
more diseases
more discontent
more unhappiness
&
more meaningless souldestroying
jobs

work

there is general misconception

amongst earth people

of this time

that all work

leads to some

net positive result

thus people toil in this world

thinking it will all lead

to something positive

for them and the future generations

only in the end

close to their death

they find

they have nothing

nothing

means

that they cannot take their

soul to a better place

they will actually go to

a lower place

coz

their net is actually in negative

they are also not leaving a better earth
for the future generations
they are leaving a ravaged polluted planet

so

work by definition
is not good by itself
as some would have you believe
workethic workculture
& other such corporate buzzwords
are continuously thrown about without
ever revealing
what exactly one is actually working for ?

only the work done
as per divine will
&
in harmony
with nature
is
fruitful
for the self and the others

the work puzzle

another of the many major misconceptions
amongst people of this planet is
that one would be free
if only one wouldn't have to work

the truth however is that
as long as one breathes
one would have to do something
it is in the nature of 'be-ing'
even if one doesn't move the body
the mind will wander
sooner or later one will move the body
to quell those desires

people will always have to work
the key is – who will they work for?
self's ambitions or divine will

people also tend to associate
freedom with just financial freedom
they only need to look
at people who have enough money
to never have to work for it again
are they happy?
they are bored and disgusted

all that they try and do
doesn't get them happiness either

'the self' cannot generate happiness
through its own efforts
without praising/serving the divine

people don't realize that
they are fed up with their jobs
only because these jobs are not
authorised by divine
these jobs are actually
against the multiversal laws/functionings
they serve a system which is inherently evil

if they choose to serve the high & divine
instead of the evil system
the work they do will automatically become pleasant
and soul-enhancing

they have slogans pasted on walls
in schools & institutions
'work is worship'
which need to be all replaced by
'work for divine is worship'

travel

qualifications are asked/required for
every activity on this planet
except for 'travel'
anyone who has enough money can travel
travel they say is meant for experiencing
but what are they really going to experience
with their limited perception/consciousness
it will all be as futile as their
travel insurance

most muggle journeys end up in
headache, stomachache & confusion
most of the time is spent waiting, getting bored
the same mundane activities
which they always indulge in, in their homes
are repeated upon reaching the destination
they come back home with some
tasteless pictures with forced smiles

muggles visit places only to
spoil them with their depression & stupidity
their muddled low vibrations are not
welcome in any nature spot
thats why the term 'touristy place'
means 'stay away from it'

travel is seen as an activity
which doesn't require skill, gnowledge or wisdom
'lonely planet' guidelines will do just fine

the west started this whole travel bug
and now the whole world is on it

the western muggles through
their own brand of mindprogramming
are never aware of their shortcomings

they think that they are
fit enough to derive enjoyment
in any place/situation/circumstance
& they try real hard
only to find the tongs of
boredom enveloping them
even tighter
they only get more suicidal after realizing
that even the best nature spots on this planet
cannot overcome the endless internal turmoil

they reach places expecting to be served
through waiving plastic cards
all they get is forced fake plastic service
where everyone is doing everything
including cooking without heart
this service couldn't/doesn't satisfy
& leaves a horrible taste in the mouth

real service only springs from
the humility one feels towards
something higher than itself

money was the tool designed by the low fallen ones
to get service
they have gotten the service
but real happiness & enjoyment
eludes them completely
all they are left with is hollow pretension

fancydress

roleplaying is one of the favourite
pastimes of the beings of this planet
&
the only preparation they seem to need for the act
is costumes

the whole scene resembles one big
purposeless fancydress party

to play a serious responsible respectable role
they put on a suit & a tie
and surprisingly the rest fall for it
hook, line & sinker
despite continuous revelations
about corrupt politicians
the fact that even mafia bosses
don expensive designer suits
doesn't dent their perception one bit

the majority of earth population
is open to manipulation through dressing

if you put on a black robe
you are a judge

if you put on a robe of any other colour
white, saffron, yellow, maroon
you are a holy man
if you put on some frills & fancy clothes
you are a rockstar
there is specific clothing
for geeks, writers, waiters ... every boxed act
there is casualwear formalwear
daywear nightwear partywear ...
funny coz most cannot carry anywear
they have no style no matter
what they wear

majority of people tend to judge others from their clothes
the being that is inside those clothes
is of no concern
in fact it is best overlooked
the prospect of really looking at someone
for what they really are
beneath the garb
is really scary
scary coz of the hideousness & monstrousness involved

no beauty to be found
when
naked in body, mind & soul

fabric

it is clear that
all signs of sense
have disappeared from
the majority of people of this planet

take their clothing for example

they have no problem donning
all kinds of synthetic unbreathable fabrics
which besides giving the
obvious sensation of itchiness
create all kinds of skin disorders

not many can be seen in
soft natural cotton
even the cotton they wear has
been put through numerous poisonous
processes and dyes

dyes are now definitely die(s)
as most of them are made up of
poisonous chemicals
poisonous to all biological functionings
including that of the body
and the environment

poisonous fabric(s) for
a society with a poisonous fabric
root of the poison being
an anti-divine stance

when one veers away from divine
first thing lost is sense
the results are clear for all to see

sense & senses

how can there be
sense
in this world
when most people
don't use their
senses
at all
they have eyes but they don't see
they can be looking straight at you
but they are not seeing you
they are practically blind
even if they started see-ing slightly
they would not do 90% of what they do

they have noses but they don't smell
(no wonder they can be sold these horrible smelling chemical deos)
they have skin but they cannot feel
(no wonder they can wear all these uncomfortable fabrics)
they have ears but don't listen
(no wonder any kind of crap noise can be sold to them as music)
they have tongues but cannot taste
(no wonder they consume all this tasteless genetically modified stuff)
...

all they do is use their mind
but mind only works from sensory inputs
they use it without using the senses
thats how it becomes sense-less
everything is just assumed, extrapolated
its like trying to solve a million piece puzzle
with 10-20 pieces
senseless

even extra sensory perception
comes from using
the senses properly first

wearing

just
wearing
the body
is
a tough-enough exercise

so its a surprise
that
most here are
more than ready to put on
more stuff
called
clothes
(unnecessarily for most part)

another simple yet clear reflection
of
their utter lack of consciousness
...

they don't even wonder
why the
word
wearing
is
same as
wear (as in wear and tear)

a modern eventline

they wear suits & ties
in warm/hot climates
then they scream for an AC
the AC air & the hot/cold variation
makes them sick
then they go to a doctor
who gives them some pills
the pills have side effects
which make them even sicker
then they take more pills
& so on and so forth

its called being
modern & civilized
after all in this world
nothing is considered more
civilized than a suit
something to cover
their gross skin fully
& a tie
dog tie

ties and watches

the 2 main emblems of evil's slavery
a tie
and
a watch

why wear a machine
right next to your skin
something which measures time
in a way very
different from
the heartbeat or breath
unless one wants to become a machine oneself
or join the borg army like darth vader
it is bad for one's physical/spiritual health
in no uncertain terms

can't be for reasons of comfort
can't be comfortable
to wear
a tie (noose) around the neck either
even animals like dogs
try to take off
the ties people
put around their neck

so even animals are
more sensitive and sensical
than so-called creatures
who pass off as human beings
people on this planet
are beyond
practicality & comfort
wearing the slave insignias
of the evil system
is more important
than anything else

the maths

the maths of peoples lives
on this planet
just doesn't add up

marijuana + yoga classes +
stressful relationship with a retarded boyfriend
+ hive functions + 9-5 grind +
self-loathing sobbing + mantra chanting

= ?

tv dinners + sodas + jogging + meditation + corporate job
+ cigarettes + gym + alcohol + love dogs + eat meat of other animals

= ?

nothing coherent
is the only answer
one can give for sure

maybe it makes sense to them
maybe they can add it up
to put 'positive numbers' in front of soul evolution

corporate

'corporate' has rightly
become a kind of swear word in the west
but in uninformed places like india
it still sadly remains a good word
in fact the only hope of a bright future

good to see the bubble burst recently
when a big IT company in India announced that it
had been fraudly showing huge profits when
it was actually functioning in loss
being so used to making-profits-from-their-little-shops mentality
they haven't quite gotten what corporatism is about

in a world where 'money' is the only 'god'
& the primary reason for doing anything
people get very startled when i say
'corporatism is not about making money at all'
its more about the pretension &
sticking people up in confined oxygenless coups called offices
making them do unnecessary things
they would rather not do
that's why they hire 10 times more people than they require
to make them do ratrace under meaningful work titles like
'assistant marketing assistant'

most major corporations in the world are in 'red'
most of the time
huge bank loans is what keeps them afloat

its all just a B-ark exercise
if anyone remembers 'hitch-hikers guide to the galaxy'
if not, its suggested that they watch the series
just to gno what 'B-ark' means
don't be shy of fastforwarding

in a nutshell its about wasting time in the most
ridiculous manner(s) possible
while inflicting maximum damage to the surroundings

the word corporate = corpo-rate = heart rate
yes heart rate
each beat wasted in orchestrated nonsense
= one less beat available for multiversal remembrance

ridicule/ous

most people are willing to go

to any extent

to not have to face ridicule from society

wear certain clothes

behave a certain way

cross the atlantic in a rowboat if they have to

to win the respect of their hive

they have no concerns however

about not having to face ridicule from divine

whatever they are doing in order to

enhance their self-image in society/system

is hilarious/ridiculous

from divine perspective

they can't be bothered as

they have no concern for

their soul or after-death state

if they decide to align with divine

they will surely face ridicule from the

unholy society/system

a straightforward choice ...

image

people
fail to realize
that
one lives (& dies) with one's self
not other people's
image
of
oneself

thus
so much
pretension
fraud
&
non-evoluting
actions

the 'like me' syndrome

there is

a massive

'like me'

syndrome

happening

on this planet

much more than any other

syndrome they talk about

you should like me

why dont you like me

people should like me

why doesn't everyone like me

all this is strange considering

that most here are just

passengers on the train to hell

why should anyone

like anyone

who is just another passenger

on the train to hell

& how would that liking help them

will that help them get off that train?

no

it would just make them

more unwilling to get off it

what is there to like in a being

who is not in control of their destiny

and just free falling into deeper hells

people of now

are asking to be liked

for just existing (that too they can hardly manage)

a very pathetic hell-bound state of affairs

why not strive to evolve one's being

to a point where

one can lead others out of hell

so that there is some point to

others liking one

instead of wanting

others to like one

even though one oneself has no clue

whatsoever

hivemind

people when quizzed deep enough
often say they don't know
why they behave like they behave
or did what they did

since everything has a reason
no matter how much one denies it
there is an explanation
and
it lies in hivementality

very few individuals walk this planet
as
very few souls are able to
step out of
the hivemind

even if they see something wrong
in the hive
they are fearful to point it out
for the fear of being excluded
this repeated lack of
straightforwardness
leads to a confused blind state
which makes it impossible to see
things as they really are

hive provides
comfort & security
very similar to a beehive
or a sheepherd

sheeps get very fearful
of being left behind in the herd
so one carries on
following hive parameters
no matter how absurd or illogical
to make sure one keeps pace

the fact that the sheep-herd
is
destined for factory knives
is overlooked
in the momentary security
&
the general umbrella for
self indulgent nonsense it provides

hivebravado

in most

the confidence to do nonsense

comes only from the

hive encouragement & security blanket

most creatures

who roar like lions

with hive backing

turn into squealing rats

when separated from the hive

when alone

people lose

most of the bravado

which made them challenge

even the divine

age of the individual

they are calling the present
as the
'age of the individual'
just because
many
can lie on a bed
laze on a sofa
talk on a mobile phone
guzzle alcohol & petrol
become a consumer of unnecessary items

they surely are unable to see
that this so-called individuation
has not made people
rise above
the mass hive muggle mentality
their perspective remains as narrow
as it ever was

just because
everyone is consuming more resources
& doing whatever the heck they fancy
doesn't make them an individual

in fact individuals
are only born out of
the decision to
serve the high & divine
to gain higher perspective

it is a step
which requires discipline
not just letting go
& going crazy
which is the current
mass definition of an individual
as seen in all their popstars/rockstars etc

different or clones ?

most people
have at least
another 100,000
exactly like them
prototype no. 1, 2, 3 and so forth

still they all believe
that they are different
or have
thoughts and emotions which
are somehow their own
and no one else's

most of their
thoughts and emotions
come from social conditioning
which is in turn controlled
by beings/forces which control society
everything about most people (muggles)
is from the same limited box

to become an individual
requires a separation
from the hive
which most are unwilling to do

to become

one of a kind

requires

proper

sadhana (penance)

which most find daunting

so

different

does require

doing really different

and evolving

even if one is born

as one of the clones

accePTance

most here seek
acceptance
from
society

only few seek
accePTance
from
higher/divine

the difference
is more marked
than between
heaven and hell

destiny or decision

lot of people
always
talk about destiny
when
everything
is
just
decisions

...

victim mentality

there is a lot of

victim mentality

going around

in this world

people are always

blaming other people

& the system

for their state

yes the system is evil

but one's own destiny

lies in one's own hands

noone can stop anyone from

praising and serving higher & divine

and raising one's soul & state

the truth is that

most people

who continuously complain about their lot in life

are not willing to take

an opportunity to change their state

even if it is presented freely

so the evil which keeps them in hell

lies as much in them

as it does in the system

the only decision

there are
only 2 sides
in this world
'divine' & 'evil'

though many want it
there is no neutral ground
those not making a clear choice
are simply on evil's side

there is no being on both sides
at the same time either
any being trying to achieve that
would only torture themselves

in this time & age
most are born
into the evil side
& have to make a clear conscious
decision
to step onto the side of divine
this step requires
humble proactivity
& a clear continuous stance

people think that
life is full of decisions
but in reality
this is the one & only decision
they have to make here

being on divine's side leads to real immortal bliss
being on evil's side leads to
boredom/emptiness/pain/torture/hells

i am (we are) like this only

'i am like this only'
'we are like this only'
phrases one gets to hear often
sometimes from the mouth
other times from the mindset
this phrase simply means
that
one is not going to change
which is only practical
if one is perfect
or one's way is perfect
is their being the way they are
leading
to bliss & happiness on all levels ?
the answer is again a simple 'no'
so this reluctance to change
is a funny thing
it simply means
one is not willing to put in the effort
to change for the better
change for the worse
is always going to happen anyways
as
change is permanent
it takes a lot of effort to
even not go down
let alone rise
clinging on to silly habits & notions
built up over lifetimes & generations
on this plane
is what makes beings
stupid
& unable to evolve
takes away the whole
point of taking birth
& being alive

hells are for ...

there is a lot of confusion
regarding hells
and who is sent there and why
so lets set the record straight
in typical lotusocean way

hells are not for
punishing
people for actions they have done

they are there for
all those
who have no intention to change
to align with multiversal laws/will
&
are full of
stubborn stupid attitudes like ...
'i am like this only'
'i don't need to change'
'i cannot change'
'what's the hurry'
'i am doing fine as i am'
'i am learning/evolving at my own pace'
etc etc ...

All People Speak Only 2 Sentences their Entire Life ...

it might seem

people are saying

a lot of things

with their

words, sentences,

body-language,

action, inaction

etc etc

but

no matter what they think

they are saying

they are always

just saying

either

'i want to go to hell'

or

'i don't want to go to hell'

Period.

the fear of ...

to
evolve
out of hell
the fear of hell
has to be more than
the fear of transformation

...

rise not fall

fall in love
they say
lotusocean says
rise in love

they have made out love to be
a pursuit of the lower
when it always really was
a pursuit of the higher

Friends & Family

the lines

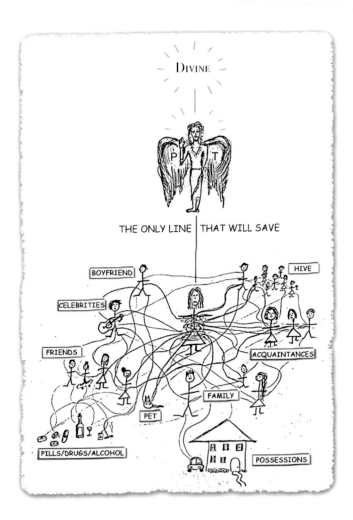

socializing

being sociable
is pushed as one of the major virtues
by the conveners of this insane theater
it is portrayed
as a fun, innocent & harmless activity
notwithstanding the fact that
in these times
socializing = surefire downfall

why? simply because
99.99% of company
one is likely to encounter
will be bad company

those who through a fear of being alone
cannot help being social
will definitely need a hive and
will as a result
have to do whatever it takes to fit in

there are too many
who despite sensory and other aversions
start
drinking beer, smoking cigs or
popping ecstasy pills
just to be part of a social scene
and
that is just the tip of the iceberg

just a warning
for those goodintentioned ones amongst you
who carefreely
walk into the dangerous web called socializing
without an inkling of the consequences
or the spiders therein

friends

'friendship' is another concept
accepted by society
& pushed vigorously by the media

but why friendship?
coz it is the best distraction
for your already dizzy attention
your friends are basically
people on a similar level to you
that don't hurt your ego
in fact
friendship is a mutual ego pampering circle

friend = free-i-end
simple put
the one who puts an end to
'a chance at freedom'

in its modern 'english' sense
it is anti-evolution
in earlier times disciples under a common guru
could be friends
they all helped each other
in a quest for evolution
the friends of today have a different role
they assist you in your quest for hell
it is a collective escape pod

friendship of today
curtails any slight chance of
the flowering of the delicate seed of individuality
it unashamedly promotes hive mind

this socalled friendship creates a blanket
which distracts one from seeing
the reality of their hellish existence
like buddh did
unfortunately he didn't have friends
so he could not just carry on smiling & laughing
he had to seek the 'truth'

not only does friendship cause one to not seek the higher
it promotes confrontation with the higher
the street gangs you see heckling people
are never just one person
people lose their head in the strength
which comes with numbers
they feel invincible

what the whole mindset is can be summed up in –
better to have company in hell
than to be alone on the road to heaven

care

those who cannot
care for their own selves
(spirit/soul, mind, body)
should not try
or pretend
to care about
any topic or subject or others
just a waste of time ...

take care / taking care

there are too many here
ready to
take care of others
when
they cant even take
care of their own
life,
body, mind, spirit,
death, future, destiny

a worldwide cliche –
parents
raising
children
when they can not seem to be able
to
raise
themselves

.

its all in the family

in these times
a
new definition
has come up for
the unit called
'family'

a set of beings
who would pay
attention only to one another
and
not to higher/divine

a simple way of
getting 'importance'
for no rhyme or reason except existing
it allows for these beings
to feel more important
than higher & divine even
within their family circle

it seems the
hiranyakashyap bug
has entered too many
only
they don't have
even the fraction of his power
still they convince themselves
to look no further
as
its all in the family

responsibility

majority of

people here

do not take

responsibility for

their own selves

otherwise

they would be

much more

response-able

(responsibility is response-ability)

to

divine

responsibility lies for the self

before being

responsible in any other way

lot of irresponsible brats

pose as responsible for family etc

being responsible for the self

is the only key

that

allows for anything/everything good to happen

in

this world and the next ...

one has to honestly face

one's irresponsibility

towards one's own self

& the extent of it

before one

can change to

being

response-able

marriage

marriage
an alchemical term
now reduced to
silly legality &
society stamps

real marriage
is between mind & heart
left side and right side
of the body
to create transformation
& in due course
enlightenment

even in the context of
a relationship between
a man and a woman
it is only real
& can only last as long
as the woman truly
finds the man higher & interesting
otherwise it is
just a sham
a charade to overcome
fear of poverty, society & loneliness
people staying together
without any real alchemy
& evolutionary goal
only leads to
bickering
conflict
depression &
devolution

the male-female completion illusion

males and females
on this planet
have the illusion that
even though they feel incomplete within themselves
once they unite
they will reach godlike completeness

this is the whole basis for
sex, relationship, marriage etc etc

it doesn't take them long to find out that
their union doesn't lead to divine bliss
in fact things just get worse
the honest admit to it others don't
but the facts & the fighting remain

its a hard pill for them to swallow that
completion they seek can only be achieved through
union with divine
not with other imperfect beings

Love

there are a lot of people running around in
this mad world spewing this word 'Love'
infact it might be the most used word
in the world, after expletives that is
even through the simplest observation we find that
this word has been reduced to a bond
pushed vigorously by media & society
created primarily between –
1. a man & a woman (lovers)
2. a woman and her child (holy mother-child relationship; we exclude
the father-child relationship here because it is not so celebrated)
3. a man and a man or a woman and a woman (friends;
gay/lesbian club takes this to the lover level)
through an honest look
one finds that ALL of these relationships
end in tears, sorrow, heartbreak
in fact most beings end up
being completely disillusioned by the whole concept of 'love'

so does True, Pure, Real, Everlasting Love exist?
and if so why do these society okayed relationships not have it?

lotusocean answers ~
YES it does exist but can only happen between
a *soul* & *the divine supersoul*
the only Love which makes sense
it is for something greater than yourself
something perfect

a Love which can actually make one transcend
all the evil of this plane
the only Love
which makes one Evolve
i.e do what Love is supposed to do

ALL the relationships of this plane are all
based on varying degrees of *selfishness*
even the love
for animals, country, religion etc is
tinged with this 'identification selfishness' which
ironically doesn't do any good for the self
though some might argue
that mother-child relationship is an exception
but it can be proven quite easily that mothers
only do something for their child as they expect
them to fulfill their own unfulfilled expectations & dreams

mothers are themselves no perfect beings
and in their ignorance push their child towards
devoluting ways without even knowing what they are doing
same applies to everyone else

how can one imperfect being Love another imperfect being perfectly ?

one can delude oneself that they do
for a while
but the illusion is likely to break

sooner or later
in ALL these relationships one
is not really loving but just expecting someone
to behave the way they want them to behave
this training in fact doesn't allow beings to
even Love the *absolute* perfectly because
they are so used to their own constructs
being fulfilled by someone else

the TRUTH is/was/willbe that only
the perfect being CAN
be loved perfectly and only that love
can lead one to perfection within
rest is just a timepass with ever-rising stakes ...
stakes are high because evil beings/demons etc
are using this word to exploit the light beings
of their soul & energy with disasterous & painful consequences
for the involved

falling in love

the people of this planet
have an expression
'falling in love'
which is quite apt
considering
they all
fall in love
not
rise in love

which is again not a surprise
considering the fact that
they are only willing to deal
with beings on a lower or same level as themselves
the net result can only be
falling
or status quo

only when one loves someone higher than oneself
does one evolve
evol-love

otherwise there is no love
just a false fake notion of it

sex
still remains
a hush hush
taboo mystery
in this world

the socalled gurus
won't talk about it
the media is loath to
mention it

its happening all over
in 1000's of twisted forms
as no one is exactly clear
what it is
or what it is for
it is the elephant in the room
which no one will address

least understood but most done
act on this planet
sex-education is just a joke
designed to introduce plastic into it

in the socalled east
it is primarily seen as a means for mindless procreation
in the socalled west
it is primarily seen as a means for frivolous recreation

the reality however is that
considering
most beings on this planet
are toxic and electrically dead

it is just a toxicity multiplier
the female will be the more affected party
considering they are
the receivers in the act

sex simply means
multiple (s) electrical charge (e) crossings (x)
its real function
as a charge (soul) enhancer
is redundant
in a world full of
electrically dead zombies

in its current form
its basically
slimy snakes slithering over each other
in a hellpit
entangling/pushing each other
further into the abyss

the responsibility of getting
electrically charged & alive
lies with the male
they need to get their kundalini active
& open up all the sacral centers
after that they can
raise the female
from the dead
since female is the receiver
it doesn't work in vice versa

the male delusion

there are no males here

they are all just females with different anatomy

despite a nagging inkling of this fact

the illusion of misplaced masculinity

keeps on pushing them to conquer

holes

making it very difficult for them

to surrender

no receiving = no evolution

all the meaningless in and outs

only increase the frustration &

notions of inadequacy

as they find themselves incapable

of achieving their objective

of establishing supremacy over the being

they are desperately trying to penetrate

a real male is like *shiv*

one who can really penetrate

one who really gnos

thus qualified for imparting

anything

from sperm to gnowledge

for the females

patriarchy & fear of women

came about on this planet

through the fear of heavy-handed matriarchy

in ancient civilizations like those of orion, alpha-draconis etc

then the patriarchy got overbearing &

gave birth to a recent phenomenon

called 'modern women's lib'

it basically was all about empowering

females through –

1. being financially independent –

which meant they do regular jobs like

males, which as one would expect

made them more butch

& eroded their femininity

so women's lib actually turned out to

be a war against femininity

it also ended up helping the evil system –

the more bodies at work the better

2. an impression was given that

a surefire way to reach equality with males was

to encourage females to do things which men do i.e

get drunk and have as much sex as they wanted

with as many as they wanted

and the females actually went out & did it

loads of sedation & pills of all kind were

required in order to do it but it was done anyways

but was there a gain

in sleeping with every tom, dick & harry?

didn't all the one night stands turn out to be

hollow gross experiences?

was anything really gained except

demeaning of one's own body/image?

women's lib. was on the surface about women's

empowerment but it was actually

about their disempowerment

the original power of women had always been there

since separation of the sexes

and it lay in

choosing which way/direction the genepool

moved/progressed

they chose who they would breed with

and in doing so they decided

which qualities would be carried forward.

this is how benegesserits control the geneflow in dune

this *choice*

was what males were always afraid of

it made the males work hard to

inculcate higher divine qualities which were more

appealing to their female counterparts

just like a peacock & not peahen works on the

plumage & dancing to make himself worthy

women basically willingly dropped themselves from this

pedestal in the name of women's lib. &

lost all grace & dignity

the more tom, dick & harrys they slept with

the more the boundaries disappeared

& the more they were willing to do anything

including commoditize/prostitute themselves

in guises of

advertising, entertainment, fashion etc. etc.

males on the other hand were/are quite happy

with the proceedings as they didn't have

to work on themselves anymore

there were enough drunken variety

of the female specie now roaming the streets &

it was hypereasy to get lucky & get laid

only quality they now needed to work on

was 'flattery' & 'superficiality'

this was helpful in women

getting fleeting temporary ego-massages but

surely was not helpful

for the genepool's evolution as the offsprings of such unions

were always going to be low quality

when a female sleeps with a male they are

basically saying to them –

we being the receptive vehicle (as nature designed)

want you to embed us i.e we want something from you

i.e the male has something important to give

any normal male gets confidence from

this 'OK stamp' – he feels he has something important to give

so females actually end up raising the

confidence of low quality males;

violence, barbarianism & devoluting stupidity follow
so women's lib. actually was
a movement for the decline & devolution
of the race through losing the
perspective of educated choice
in ancient vedic tales, the women usually
chose their husbands in a ceremony
called *'swayamvar'*
they basically chose
whoever they thought was the best specimen
or didn't choose any if they thought
no one was good enough
that to me was real women's lib
its only since the dark ages set in did the concept
of arranged marriages arise in the east
in the west the women lost all discrimination
an easy thing to do when you are
doing all the nonsense that men do with equal gusto
now the situation has reached
such a level that even 14–15 year schoolgirls
look weary and worn out through
behaving like professional prostitutes
i don't see any empowerment in this
its just an easy descent into the abysses
of hell ... the only way out –
restoration of dignity
through self-discipline &
pursuit of the higher ...

the chase & chaste

females on this planet
have become so used to
being chased
rather than chase themselves
to the extent that
most have completely forgotten
how to chase

in all vedic tales
even the goddesses
like *parvati*
concentrated on chasing
rather than being chased
parvati chased *shiv*
which is the more sensible thing to do
no matter how one looks at it –
one wants to evolve
or have a better time
or have a more interesting existence
or have bliss

females who settle for those who chase them
cannot/donot ever end up on the bliss-side
it is no coincidence
that the word 'chaste' is connected to 'chase'
only a female chasing the higher/divine
can truly be chaste

whether one is a male or female
one will have to chase the higher/divine
as higher/divine is
the only gateway
for one to evolve

special

my cat/dog/pet is special
my boyfriend is special
our connection is special
what is special
one asks
other than they exist
& have limited consciousness

no answer
except it is their choice
so whatever they choose is special
because they are so special
they are not just a
depressed being
feeling like a prisoner of circumstance
all the time
they are special
& by default
all occasions they are involved in are special
not just a boring meaningless unfractal disaster

there are some who ask me to
see how everyone is special (including them ofc)
not just me
another roundabout way of aiming at equality
which is not the reality

what that special is
they can't themselves put their finger on
the word is now in hyperoveruse
any gremliny idiosyncracy
or inclination towards self-torture
or bad habits or brattiness or idiocy
is termed as special

how are they different from
all the half-dead mindprogrammed hellbound zombies here ?
can they even inhabit the heart of their own sun ?
most won't even gno what that is
or where to begin
but they are all special

in time before the current age of utter stupidity
where mere existence
while going on a downward spiral is special
beings used to
develop their soul
through penance and devotion to divine
gaining many real powers in the process
only then did they come
to be gnown as a *rishi* (seer)
or someone special

the social worker

those who can't help themselves
are always found distracting themselves
trying or pretending to help others
whenever they confront something
better than oneself
the social worker inside gets edgy
service by their definition
can only be done for the inferior
not the superior
no chance of ever serving divine on this path
coz divine will always be superior

service of the higher
is the path of evolution & bliss
service of the highest
is perfection

pathetic

whenever confronted with something higher
than oneself
it is easy to realize the patheticness of one's own being
that is not a bad thing in itself
as it creates room for humility
but the really pathetic part is the
majority's response to this feeling
they immediately look for something
more pathetic than themselves
and keep company with it
to feel good about themselves

the door firmly shut
on evolution
devolution here we come
its all worth it
as long as
the ego is safe

dog-god polarity

its not a coincidence that
dog and god
are reverse of each other

its either seeking of
the superior/divine/god
for getting out of hell
or
egoboosting thru the inferior/dog
& continuing to suffer in hell

it must be noted that
the term 'dog' does not
always refer to the canine animal
... dogs come in various
species/shapes/sizes/forms !

love & service

to
completely
disassociate
the word
love
from
service
as many have done
for various stupid reasons
is absolutely ridiculous

love and serve
are inseparable
love without service
is just madness and devolution
without evolution love is nothing
as
love is short form of evol-love only

serving
higher and divine
shows
one
has
love
for
oneself
&
without
love for
one's own self
no other
kind of love
is possible

twice born

first birth is from the
physical mother
that everyone has
very few gno or aspire
for anything else
thus remaining firmly tied in the
knots of dependency and obligation

there is however
a second birth
not an outof
but an into birth
it is a birth
into divine
divine becomes
the mother, father, everything after that
no obligations
remain to the physical mother, father
relations etc etc

only when one is twice born
does one become a *brahman*
a gnower of *brahmgyan* (multiversal gnowledge)
truely free

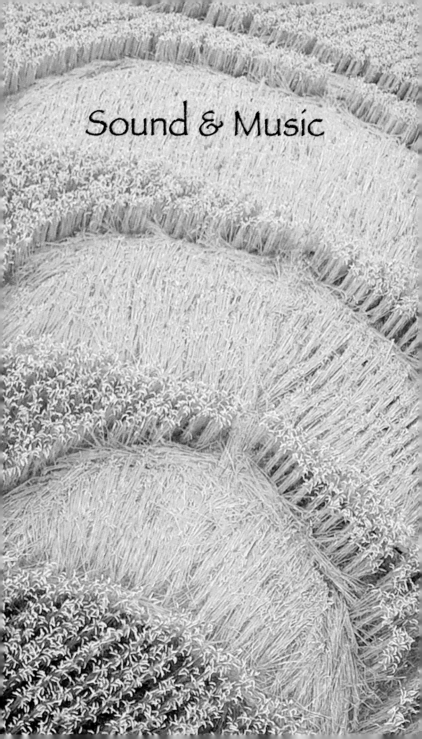
Sound & Music

Saaouund

when people listen to music
they don't realize that
their attention usually
concentrates on either
the vocals, the beat or the tune
but all these 3
just act as distractions from
the real element – saaouund
thats why many get away
with poxy, plasticky, annoying digisounds
through the use of
repetitive hypnotic loops
called 'tunes' or
verbal diarrhea called 'lyrics'
its like selling a worthless
product through clever packaging
the sounds which most of
so-called musicians
use are useless for the soul

a saaouund exploration ~
Shravan ~ Shatabhisha
youtu.be/0E4Ta5OO1-A

LotusOcean Radio

there are a lot of radios
blaring sounds out there
to drag each & every one towards
hell & hellish states
so here are some sounds
from lotusocean
for doing just the opposite

RadiostationPT:
http://radio.lotus-ocean.net/

the real stairway to heaven
sounds to clean your mind/consciousness
ofc only if you approach
them with respect & receptivity

if you do
we can promise
your ears will never be the same again

LotusoceanRadio youtu.be/0E4Ta5OO1-A

rainmaking

in ancient times
music was not a disconnected
separative entity
to broadcast one's immature depression

it was connected with the
pulse & vibration of the multiverse &
the elements
real music when played properly
could thus invoke rain
or make it disappear
depending upon the intention

Creating Storms the Size of Continents youtu.be/PU3zX18yQZU
Nilgiri Rainmaking youtu.be/eba3PUjp-iw
RainMaking youtu.be/UT39bywwzUU

rock 'n' roll

real rock 'n'roll
is about having
individuation & independence
its about taking responsibility for
one's own self
self being the body, mind, spirit/soul trinity
it takes lots of
discipline, learning attitude & gnowledge
to get there

the prevalent publicized globalized version
which has idols
who are basically suicidal
and do not take any responsibility for the self
is not rock 'n' roll
that rock is never gonna roll

real rock 'n' roll
is only by higher/divine
which can actually take one higher ...

Gaudhuni P-art-y ~ one man band <u>youtu.be/z1NeYUYMAuE</u>

electric guitar & electric bodies

even though muggles
should lay off all instruments
electric guitar is something
they should completely avoid

the chances of making bad sounds with it
are enormous
as in the realm of electricity
the sound choice is enormous
wider aural spectrum to mess with ='s
greater aural damage

electric guitar/amplifiers/effects
only amplify the incoherence within
most produce mosquito buzzes
& jerky hiccupy wailing

usually they hide the electric guitar
behind bass/drums/vocals
that's what producers/mixing engineers
have done since the 1950's

there has been no person
who has been able to
handle this instrument solo
that includes all the socalled guitar heroes
& the millions trying on youtube

to maintain continuity & coherence
on an electric guitar
requires one's own electrics
i.e kundalini to be working properly

it is a magical device
with complicated almost quantum possibilities
in terms of
tones, overtones, harmonics, resonance, feedback etc.
not an instrument for
staggering
back from the pub folks

if played properly
a single electric guitar
can produce more complex sounds
than a whole orchestra
while taking the whole thing
into another dimension

its not about moving your hands & fingers madly
which all muggles think guitarplaying is about
its about sound & holding the wave

one's level of evolution shows through
everything one does
but with more loud powerful electrical tools
it is all hyper-magnified

and if one cannot handle electric guitar properly
how is one going to handle another body
which is basically
all electric (nerves, brain) in nature

singing

there are lots of attempts at singing
by various genepools here on earth

from an objective outsiders look
it is seen that
most of these genepools haven't
even learned to speak properly
i.e speak from the center of their mouths
they all speak in lopsided twisted ways
either to the left or to to the right
if you don't believe
switch on the telly
and start paying attention

toddlers learn to walk before they run
but here people learn to sing
before they can speak

all twisted & annoying wailing, screaming
passes off as singing as long as
it aims to hit some funny intervals called notes

no intonation or mantric power
in the voice
is seen as a requirement for singing
in fact it is taboo
to be that impactful
singing is afterall just one part of
the light entertainment circus

'gnoing' is also not seen as having any relation with 'the voicing'
despite the fact that all tales tell an opposite tale
'the voice' of benegesserits in dune
which can command or
'the voice' of sages in the puranas
which has a direct soul impact
anything real with any power has to be avoided
simply coz its not something one can relate to ...

in tune ~ sur asur

being in tune
has nothing to do with
being in tune
with the
frequency intervals called musical notes

it is however all to do with
being in tune
with the multiversal divine source

thats why
'sur', the sanskrit term for 'tune'
is replaceable
for
the 'devas' or
the good godly folk
while 'asur' meaning 'not in tune'
is used for demons
suggesting that they are so
because of not
being in tune
with the divine will

the new flute ~
herding souls back home

some ask
what is the point of
PT's music

many among those have
read/heard Krishn's tales of playing flute
to herd the गौ (cows) back home
these cows are busy munching
immersed in
the various herbs/grasses/leaves
of the jungle
and have lost all sense of anything
else beyond that

people don't question the point in
this exercise in the story
'cows have to be brought back home'
it all sounds obvious and natural to them
but they miss the real point of
which this story is only the metaphor

sanskrit गौ 'gau' has two meanings
cow & the senses
it is 'the senses' meaning which is crucial
the senses are always wanting to
feed upon the various things
in the jungle of this world
it takes divine sound to
grab their attention
which inturn allows
them to come back to the
real home
home of divine

that's what PT's lotusocean sounds
are for –
herding
souls back to the source
guitar is the new flute
of this time
only the sounds matter –
flute is just a metaphor
for an instrument
and electric guitar
is the instrument of choice for now

only the avatar music
can enchant them out of this world's offerings

if cows have to come home
don't the souls ?

Learning
&
Education

people are strange

the strange bit about
the people of this planet
is not
how little they actually gno
it is
how little they actually want to learn

qualified

beings
on this planet
find themselves
not qualified
for a lot of
things/activities
without appropriate training etc
but
surprisingly
they all
feel qualified
for surfing the timewave
called life
without any
training
preparation
gnoing

...

no research

there have been

so many theories

to explain

the dumbness and retardedness

of the muggles who make up the majority of the masses

but they hardly ever get to the PoinT

which is that people are dumb like they are

because they have an inherent

non-researching attitude

and

just to clarify for all muggles

research does not mean phd. from

any silly so-called university

re-search is the

re - again

search

for

core existential answers

no research

leads to 2 things

1. monkey see monkey do approach of getting through life

2. seeking attention for oneself for no rhyme or reason

both of which lead to

being trapped in the matrix

which in turn means

boredom, hell & torture

the Absolutely Rarest thing ...

having surveyed

this world

and its inhabitants

Lotus Ocean

has found

that the

Rarest thing here

is

not Gold or Diamonds

or Uranium ...

the Rarest thing

(insert drum rolls and all ...)

is

(insert loud guitars and all ...)

Learning

Attitude

youth - yis or yes

most on this planet
suffer
from
what can be called as
muggle 'youth invincibility syndrome' - YIS
they are always far away from
YES - youth enquiry sense

when people reach that age
of 16/17
they get carried away by
a torrent of energy called youth
which they find themselves unable to cope with
its too intoxicating a drink for them
it makes them
heady, proud, non-listening
they all seem to gno what to do
without having any
real gnowledge at all

learning, humility
all seem like bad words
old age seems like something
which only happens to others
death does not even exist

it seems youth is what they are
born for again and again
but cannot really utilize anytime

miseducation

education is a big word
in this world
when none is actually happening

the so-called educators
going under the accepted social term 'teachers'
gno nothing themselves
but have assigned themselves the role
to set up curricula, tests &
environments for learning

under the banner of change & improvement
one encounters jokers
who aim to breathe life into
this fundamentally faulty & dead system
where instead of evolution
jobs & fitting in is the key
they consider themselves
experts on what is good for kids and others in general
without being sure about
what is good for themselves

the fact is that
in countries like india
where education is the buzzword
it is way more difficult to talk sense
with an educated person
than with an uneducated villager

belief in temples is dying but
the belief in
schools, colleges and universities
shows no signs of abating

education in its current context
is simply a conveyer belt
to churn out slaves for a borg system
all its grandiose institutions
consuming enormous resources
are no different from waste landfills

this pseudoeducation doesn't tackle
any real issues like
life or death
what else is there anyways

school

there is a phenomenon
on this planet
called school
supposedly meant for teaching beings

it doesn't teach beings
how to sit properly
how to speak properly
how to live properly
how to evolve one's soul

then what does it teach
one wonders
it teaches
swearwords, gremlininess
through providing a common ground for
interaction with other spoilt brats

all it does is prepare
them for being part of
the mindless system
through
stuffing them up with
incoherent data

still every parent
wants to send their progeny to it
& there are many who think
school system can be improved
that it is not essentially flawed

they took the guru out of the
gurukul system of learning
to create s-kul (s-kool)
they replaced guru with s for system
a system which appointed
multiple unaware teachers
to setup
an assembly line
producing unhumble robotic zombies
serving evil & hurtling headlong
down the conveyer belt to hell

teachers

many are given this title of 'teacher'
in society
none of them
having the slightest clue
about even the
T in T-each
T being the crossing for 'each' soul

still these
well-respected members of society
do this pretend game
of gnoing and teaching
every day
surely as or more evil a deed
than any so-called criminal does

education

people of this planet
send their children to
schools and universities
for education
the thinking is that
they would learn something

they are (like all else) totally oblivious to the fact
those places exist
for making sure
beings don't come to gno anything
while instilling the false idea
that they gno a lot

...

real student

only
when the
discontent
with
the 3-d matrix
one's own state
& mad society of the present
gets more than
one's ego
is one ready to
be a real student

it doesn't happen
from being forced into so-called schools
wearing the school uniforms
entering buildings called universities

it happens from
an urgent realization
something has to be done

questions

there are those who think
that they can learn/acquire gnowledge
by just asking questions
to whoever/wherever/whenever

they have no idea
that one has to earn the right
to ask a question
for the answer to have any
actual lasting significance in their life/afterlife

under-standing happens only
through standing under
not asking questions

they are aware that they have to do some actions
just to survive in this world
but for learning
they feel all that is required is
mouthing/typing a question

a funny attempt at completely eliminating
the immortal & logical guru-disciple concept
based upon secure foundations of
humility & service

all this has happened
from the myths propagated by the west
to promote brattiness (one whines for an icecream and gets it)
that everyone deserves everything

& thus
everyone has a right to access
all the multiversal gnowledge

but that would never be the case
beings will only have access to as much gnowledge
as they deserve

thats why most beings here
gno less than 2%
about the reality of this world's system
they put their faith in and work for
let alone multiversal functionings

right has to be right

to those who think
that it is their
right to ask questions
by just the mere act of existing

lotusocean informs that

only right they have
is to praise/serve something
higher than themselves

coz it is the only right thing to do

the incompleteness of
the reading/writing method

those who think that they can
learn something just by silent reading
are under a big illusion

learning only happens through
verbal repetition
(internal for the mute, external for the rest)
repeating
just as the guru (teacher) has spoken

the way guru said something
was as important as what he/she said

even this only worked
if the basic requirement –
'praise, respect and service to the guru'
was satisfied

this was the vedic way of teaching
employed since beginning of time
why?
it was simply the only way that actually worked
through wholistically covering all the bases

reading and writing promoted mindlessly in
today's schools and institutions
has no chance of imparting any learning
which can assist in soul evolution

even those reading these scriPTures
will not really learn anything
which they can practically instill into their lives
to evolve their soul
until they have the discipline to do
continuous verbal repetition of the text
+ respectful service to the guru

who'll teach who

there are lots of symptoms
given for
kaliyug – the dark age
in vedic scriptures
but one main attitudinal point which is often
missing from all sources
is this –

when the lower boldly & shamelessly
try to teach & preach to the higher
instead of humbly learning
kaliyug has reached its zenith

and like all things nondivine
with *kaliyug* the end is very near the zenith

the biggest delusion

the biggest delusion
evil has propagated on this planet

is

that

'learning is possible'
without bowing to higher/divine

so one can learn from
books, articles & internet
without ever being
humble & of service to the teacher
who by definition
has to be more evolved than themselves

thats why all
who are deluded by this delusion
languish in
depths of blissless boredom
of the hell that is their life

& will

for eternity
if they stick to this delusion

there are those who are proclaiming
that 'life/time is the greatest teacher'
if that was the case

all would be enlightened by now
as each & every person's family/forefathers
have been on this planet for
thousands of years
the same genetics
have gone through life
over & over & over ...
without ever getting out of
mind-programmed hell
they have been stuck in

there are those who think
learning is possible through
combined effort of
many incoherent beings
but sum of incoherence never added upto coherence
simple mathematics can reveal that fact
$-12 + -4 + -8 + ... = -$ a lot instead of a '+'

all ancient scriptures
especially vedic puranas
point towards
learning happening only through
bowing/service to the real learned rishis (seers)
& direct manifestations of divine

G~uru

guru
a grossly misused term in these times

there are so many
gurus of this and that

in real terms
there is only one type of
guru
&
that is for evolution

'g' for gene/gravity
'uru' for serpent
thus
g-uru is
the one
who raises
the gene serpent up

there is a lot of gravity
to this term
its not to be taken lightly
as it is nowadays
otherwise suffering will be the result

the guru twist

in ancient times
guru's purpose was
ensuring evolution
through a continuous 24/7 involvement
with the disciple's life

these days 'guru' has been
reduced to
a seal of approval for
whatever you wanna do

if one looks at
all the so-called gurus
who have been accepted
in the west
from 'osho' to 'amma'
one finds that they all
allow people to do anything
that they want
i.e don't interfere with their lives
no discipline or change
required for evolution

'the beatles' go to the fraudo mahesh yogi's ashram
for a few months

& within a twinkling of an eye
they are back to
their ham, alcohol & business
mahesh yogi is happy with the publicity & donations
they are happy with the illusion
of being spiritually blessed

people are not looking for change or evolution
they just want to keep on living
their lives in the hell they have created
spirituality to them is just a concert
they want to attend every now and then

they don't need a guru
they need a sycophantic performer
to tell lies
about them and their future

a real guru they do not deserve
simply bcoz
they are not seeking the higher
also
they won't have the slightest idea
how to treat one

older & elder

even though most people
automatically (& erroneously) consider
older as elder
the fact is that
there is a big difference
between
older & elder

older just means more age
i.e more earth years in a physical form
while
el-ders are those
who have
their
el

el

turning serpent
kundalini
working
and all the chakras flowering

so when they say respect the elders
it doesn't mean you respect
your parents and uncles and aunties
it means
that you
respect the
awakened beings

discipline/disciple

discipline is losing the battle
in a world where all the media
is screaming/preaching loudly – 'be undisciplined'
its cool & great to have that coffee or toffee
you are indestructible & no harm can come to you
most people have a fear of discipline
from the trauma they carry from the silly school discipline
which is designed to artificially fit one into society
no matter how they all try and run away from
any kind of discipline
they find they run straight into it
the school is followed by 9-5 jobs
the same society
which blatantly propagates undiscipline
puts people in cages for 8-12 hrs a day
to toil for an undisclosed goal
even basic disciplines like eating home-self-cooked-proper food
are disappearing fast
along with them will disappear
respect for the higher
the more undisciplined one is
the more unable one is to respond properly to the higher
such beings end up becoming vampiric apathetics
for them the energy of the higher is too much to handle
so they end up
criticizing, swearing, pointing fingers and shunning it instead
no discipleship without discipline
there is a reason why these 2 words are the same
di-sci-p-line
diverse branching/cutting of P(the axis) line
in simpler terms
one has to have discipline at every turn
to navigate properly
through the phenomenon called life

a real student/disciple

a real disciple is one
whose ears just listen to the guru
whose mouth just praises the guru
whose attention is fixed positively on the guru

also

the guru chosen
should be higher than oneself
for it to be any real guru-disciple relationship
which will take one closer to the divine

some can choose to make
divine itself their guru
the same principles apply

Spirituality
&
Evolution

spirit & soul

the 2 words
spirit & soul have become synonymous
amongst people of this planet
they see no difference
between them

spirit however
is not the same as soul

many beings here
don't have a 'soul'
they have a spirit
the talk that every being
with a nose, 2 eyes
walking on 2 feet has 'soul'
is nonsense

. thats why there is so much talk
of **spirit-uality**
& not much mention
of **soul-ality**

technically the difference between
spirit & soul
comes from level of coherence

the word 'soul

comes from 'sol'

or 'sun'

the beings

who can generate their own light

through connection with

the divine supersoul

are the ones who have soul

(not many of them here)

the rest are just spirits

who can under certain conditions

generate a soul

depending on their efforts

to establish/re-establish

connection with

the divine supersoul

the Primary

majority

of people

here

are very into the

peripheral

secondary

&

tertiary

...

but

they

have

little or

no interest

in the

Primary

thus all the frustration

and madness

as they wonder/scream

why

nothing ever really works out for them

Primary
has the root
Prime
for a reason
and
Prime
has
the
root
P
for a
reason

...

attention

there are widespread notions that
one owns their body, thoughts, emotions,
cars, houses etc etc
but the truth is that
one's attention is all one owns
and it should be used
to focus on divine & its activities
this makes the attention pure, free and undivided
the result of which is a permanent bliss state

the most fatal mistake
in soul evolution
a spiritual aspirant can do
is to put one's precious attention
on one's own self
i.e body, thoughts & feelings
mirrors have to be discarded
both external and internal

this is completely opposite to
what all the faulty systems
have been deluding people with
telling them to self-reflect
focus/analyse their own
physical responses, thoughts, feelings
basically getting them more and more entangled
in the unfractal spider web of pain & unhappiness

the most obvious thing

people seem
perennially confused
about
how their self will improve
and
most try to
improve it by putting focus/attention on the self
but that
(obviously) never works
and all they end up with is
frustration

self can only improve
when one can
put focus/attention
on
the most obvious thing
&
that is the
blaring shining
higherness
of
higher & divine

only that awareness
and
holding that awareness
second to second
can
raise one
higher

ATTENTION

attention

can

be used

2 ways

either

it

can be put on

one's own self

and

cause all kinds of complications/grief

or

it

can be put out onto

something much more

interesting

i.e

higher & divine

and

create bliss

which is more natural ?

a no-brainer

...

this is the basic root decision

everyone here

has to make

pun, fun & evolution

many souls are often turned away
from the evolutionary path
coz
there is a deliberate artificial schism
created between
fun & **evolution**

evolution is portrayed as a boring process
much like school
while drunk gyrating in a dingy night club
is the definition of fun
the reality is the absolute reverse
every step taken towards divine
creates real bliss & consequently more fun

the advertized packaged definitions of fun
as conjured up by evil's minions
are a pun on fun
they lead to absolute boredom
which in turn leads to
dependency on alcohol & drugs
the final price is the soul itself

blame must also go to the
ugly blissless self-appointed
heads of spirituality

who through their sheer ignorance
propagate dull, dour, turgid & uncool
processes
that hold no appeal to
any youngster
searching for cool

as a result
youngsters fail to realize that
divine is more rocking than any rock band
it is infinitely more cool & groovy too ...

future

it should be

automatic

and

reasonable

for all

beings

to

care about their future

but

strangely

one finds not many really do

some just think about immediate future

but thinking is different from caring

which is an action-oriented term

and

caring of many

just extends to insurances and such

really caring about future

actually extends from

now

to

eternity

the basic question

the basic question
which any person
needs to ask themselves
is this –

would i be fine
with having
the life which i have gotten this time
(from very infancy to now)
again in the next birth

if the answer is 'yes'
the same question should be asked for
a life worse than one has had
and so on
till one says 'no'
such people
no matter how reluctantly
will have to make some effort to learn
about what not to do to
not fall below their own
self-defined low standard

if the answer to the above question is
'no' straightaway
such people should

become eager and ready to learn
what will make sure that doesn't happen

any so-called spiritual mumbo-jumbo which
people try and do around the world
without asking and answering this question
is all nonsense
and can/will never bear fruit

those whose answer is that
they don't want a life here again period
are on their way to real spirituality
such beings are the only ones
who can sincerely & fully turn to divine

those who say
they do not care what life they get next
well
can carry on their merry mindless way
into hell & torture

goals

it goes without saying
that one's efforts are always towards one's goal
lets look at the kind of goals beings here are setting themselves
as kids it is all about plastic toys
as teenagers its all about parties
as adults its all about gaining as high a position in
society as they can

very few beings here are even contemplating
goals like
breaking out of *mrityulok* (3-D matrix)
not having to be born here again
in the temporary realm of pain & disease

this is the case

even when they are living in times where

all the pain & suffering of their own and others

is all very clear and out in the open

almost everyone from a sportsperson to a housecleaner gnos

that a goal has to be set first

before any effort can be made to reach it

most are hyperbusy setting & achieving meaningless temporary goals

as soap-bubble-superfluous as

the zillions of silly new year resolutions

surprisingly there is also no real change in goals

despite all the bubble bursting

which always happens in time

the happiness they expect at the moment of reaching their goal

never materializes

whether it be the top of mount everest

or holding the trophy they wanted most

thousands of goals have already been scored in football

but the heavens haven't opened up as yet

at the end of the day

the only difference between all beings

is what goals they set for themselves

survival or servival

majority
on this planet
are focussed on just
'survival' with a 'u'

with this very limited aim and attitude
even if one does survive
till death
of what use is it
as one will be thrown back in
this world to begin the gruesome
struggle for survival again

what is the point of sustaining the body
if one has no clear goal
as to what one would do with the body
which would take one out of
the hellish cycle of 3-d existence

the real spelling
is actually
'servival'
one is here to serve divine
not just survive
survival is automatic
if one serves divine
thats why the real word is
'serve-i-val'
serving i value

service compendiums

lets deal with another
swearword in modern parlance
'servant'
which is deemed okay in reference to
made-up inanimate collective franchises like a
football club, company or government
but a complete no-no when
used in context of individual dealings

the ancient vedic literature
called *Puranas*
which the epics *Mahabharat* and *Ramayan*
are a part of
can easily be called
'Servant/Service Compendiums'
to make them relevant in today's world

they are all primarily aimed at
showing how one should serve the
higher & divine

whether it be *Hanuman* serving *Ram*
or *Kunti* serving *Durvasa*
or various disciples serving their respective gurus

the primary emphasis of today's world
is to get
as far away from
the servant/serving state as possible
thats why the peasants are trying to become
govt. officials and corporate ceo's

only to find that they end up serving
something or the other
not necessarily higher than them
in terms of soul evolution
to put it straight
they end up serving the evil demiurge

this obviously has been propagated from
what is now called 'the west'
where the whole servant compendium was
limited to
'how to be a butler'
but the butler archetype was no real servant
as it expected things in return like pay etc
and was many a times smarter than its master

the hierarchical system propagated by the west
was not based on soul evolution
which was a given
considering that they occupied a very low position in
spiritual hierarchy

instead of humbly rising upwards
they decided to turn it upside down
and put themselves on the top
by simple methodologies like 'divide & rule' &
setting up money systems completely under their control
to make others serve them
they conveniently forgot that
any upside down system has its fatal repercussions
& a time limit
the sand is running out ...

ParamounT

action

is

ParamounT

control of action

action

can

only

be

controlled

through

an

alternative

action

not

through

attempts

at

cessation

of

action

through

meditation

or any such

ACTION

the

word / term

'action'

has a very different

meaning

now

when

compared

to

what it has always

actually meant

from the

beginning

of

creation

action for those

trapped in

mass muggle consciousness here

has nothing to do with

'consequences'

or

'continuity'

or

'coherence'

action

to them

is some

general whimsical

meaningless

scattered disconnected

burst of energy called activity

which doesn't have to

last through time

do one

then do another

and so forth

no coherent context required

no sense of consequence

well such a

definition of

action

can only

lead to

lowering of consciousness

and

descent into deeper hellishness

and

what do we see all around

here ...

heaven & beyond ...

the sanskrit word for

heaven is

स्वर्ग

swarg

which means

swa - self (sustaining)

rg - fire

ie.

self-sustaining phire

so how does one get

this self-sustaining fire ?

since it has to be sustained by self

lets see what is in

self's hands ?

actions

now for sustainability

actions would have to be

right / correct / perfect

so what is right action ?

eating / living right is an obvious answer

but the definition of right in all that

can get very complicated

so what is a simple yet always right/correct/perfect action ?

praising/serving higher & divine

is the most right action

which is accessible to anyone

does not require any special skill or gnowledge

just a desire to evolve (get out of hell)

& an attitude of service

to

reach heaven & beyond ...

cognisance

all the people
are doing actions
on this planet
as one can not exist without
doing some kind of action
but hardly any
are
cognisant of their actions
and one
cannot do right actions
without being fully cognisant
of one's actions

they dont take a moment to ask
where am I ?
who am i with ?
what am i doing ?
is it worth doing ?
what will be the result ?
will it evolve me ?

if people just started
taking responsibility for their
body & actions
a lot would improve
very quickly
in this world

wording it as it is

people here
need to
word things
as they really are

'i have a right to jump into a one-night stand'
i have a right to jump into hell

'i am going to the pub'
i am going to hell

'i want to teach/write without gnoing anything'
i want to go to hell

etc etc.

if one still does it
that's upto one
but
the wording has to be clear
for one's own clarity
otherwise
one will go to hell
and not even gno
how/why one got there

...

only one kind of seriousness

seriousness
is
not
depression
graveness
solemness
humourlessness
quietness
or many other 'nesses
as many tend to perceive

there is only one kind of
seriousness
and
that is care and concern
for one's future
not just immediate future
or future till death
but
all future existence in toto
beyond this life & death

a real concern about not
never ever
getting into bad situations,
ignorance, pain
entrapment

a being without
this seriousness
is a being without any base
or foundation

and
cannot be dealt with
in any meaning-full way

such a life is a waste
no real learning or
pleasure or bliss or
evolution is possible

the fear

people have no fear
of their self
directing their life
no matter how many bad situations
the self leads them into
but there is immense
fear of
being directed by
a higher force, being or divine

on the highway of life
they are ready to crash the car
any number of times
& reach deadends after deadends
rather than giving the steering
to someone who gnos the way
& how to drive

what is the body for ?

there are many people
on this planet
doing many strange things with their body
twisting & turning it about
putting all kinds of substances in it
treating it like a rental car
without ever asking the basic question
what is the body for ?

the body is like a bow
to the arrow that is the soul
the DNA in your genes
is the slinky
which shoots up your soul
at the moment called death

just like an airplane requires
adequate velocity (speed) to take flight
in the same way the
soul requires
adequate velocity
(faster than speed of light)
to break through the matrix of this plane

so if one does not train
one's body/dna
to do that
through praise/service to divine
it is the waste of a body

goes without saying
one gets a worse model each time
one misuses

the vow to evolve

people take many
vows
but
very few take the
vow to evolve

those who don't
take this vow
will always devolve

evolution is not automatic
it doesn't happen by just existing
or in time
as darwin may have some believe

there is no
evolving by chance
&
there is no
neutral ground
of stasis

it will always
be
up or down
and
for those who
are not fully committed
to evolving
it will
just be down

evolution is the only revolution

some ask
what is the point of evolution ?
why be so concerned about it ?
well
if one is fine
doing what one does not want to do
if one is fine
being a slave to an evil system
if one is fine
being helpless
if one is fine
with things not going their way
if one is fine
being blissless in hell
then there
is
actually no need to worry
about evolution
but once you have made the decision
do not complain about
your job, your boss,
your boring life
your pathetic existence

if you however
Do want to
break free of the matrix prison
you would need to evolve
there is no other r-evolution
which can save you
revolution is just real evolution

& for evolving
you will have to
be respectful to higher/divine

addiction

what is
addiction
but
a
lack of
diction

(*a* is always a 'negative'
as in *dharma* – righteousness
and *adharma* – unrighteousness)

most people
right now
are sidey
and have bad/improper
diction

no wonder
all ancient
Vedic gurukuls
just mainly concentrated
on
getting
diction
right

so-called schools and universities
of right now have teachers
who have no clue as to
what proper centered diction is

so its no surprise
addiction is rife

Path

there are those
who try to hide behind
complications
& say that
there are many paths

the reality is that there is only
1 Path (P-ath)
with
its normal
2 directions
one going away from divine and
one going towards divine

तपउस्या ~ tapasya

through movies & media
people of this planet
have been programmed
to think
that power comes from
going to gym
&
lacing oneself with metal & technology

the truth is that
DNA/soul is not enhanced but
perturbed by this

real power/bliss comes through *tapasya*
(penance being the closest term in english)
& only *tapasya*
is
praising high & divine

anything

you can do anything –
earn as much money as you want
have a full cover life insurance
have savings for your old age
eat spirulina or vegan food
hug trees
hug each & every person on the street
cry & laugh & sing & dance
join alternative communities
wear any amount of outfits
go to any concert/festival/seminar
get/give as many awards & titles
draw, paint, write
have one night stands
have many night stands
cling on to each other
jump & shout
create or procreate
meditate or mediate
hold conversations & debates
get on stage or a reality show
live in the limelight or under the radar
live in the mountains or near the sea
work hard or laze around
drive any car
take all the pills & chemicals
research old bones or new science
eat all the chocolates
drink all the cocktails
join yoga classes

hit the gym
travel to any part of the world
read all the books there are
see all the movies there are
play all those scenes in your life
kiss, hurt, kill, save

you still won't get out of
the blissless hell
that you're in
& have no clear gnoing of where
your soul is headed for after the shedding of the body

in fact you won't move
even an inch forward in soul-evolution terms
with each action you do
you will sink deeper
into the hellswamp
its better to stay completely still (impossible to do)
when you're sinking
but that also just delays the inevitable

death is no escape either
coz it takes you to even more harsher hells
only to bring you back to square one

unless you
stop 'doing' as per your self's direction
& surrender &
actually/practically
bow down to
the higher & divine
there is no escape
period

Essential

so
what is
really
essential

once again
meaning is the word
beyond the spelling

e-ssential

e-cent-ial

e-center-i-align

bringing
energy
to the center
to Praise higher/divine
is
the
only
real
ESSENTIAL

medicine

so what is
medicine

answer to that
lies in another question

why
is
there
a
medi
in
medi-cine

medi
='s middle
='s center

its clear
centering
is
the
only
real
medicine
as
in
medi-tation
etc etc

the most natural thing

after a mass epidemic of un-naturality
natural is
becoming a 'buzzword'
once again
on this planet

however
most don't realize that the
most
basic primary seed/root impulse
upon which
this multiverse stands/functions
is
the impulse
one feels to
behave
properly
in front
of
higher
&
divine

its more natural
than lets say
the impulse to
not eat thorns

when this
root naturality goes
all other natural sense
is bound to leave one
and
all hells follow as a result ...

Right Behaviour

the thirst

having an overwhelming

thirst

for

getting out of this 3-D plane existence

getting real gnowlege about this multiverse

getting to higher planes after death

getting close to divine

is essential

for any being to behave correctly

& make use of their life here

this thirst cannot be

given to anyone

one has to feel it oneself

quite easy to do

in the desert that is this world

those who have it

don't waste their time

doing/saying nonsense

those who don't

well ...

BEHAVIOUR

so why
are all these beings
stuck here
in such a bad situation
&
don't have access to higher realms

well
the answer
doesn't require whole libraries full of books
it is quite simple

~

BEHAVIOUR

~

they just don't gno how to behave
in front of
Higher & Divine

~

the current school, society, system
teaches them
all the wrong ways of behaving
&
their bratty selves are more than happy
to learn and apply those wrong behaviours
which take them straight to hell

...

so to get out of hell
one has to learn
how to Behave

...

Behave to BeHave youtu.be/DyGHAnq5mzY

good and bad qualities

there is a whole lot of
discussion and confusion regarding
what exactly are good (positive) qualities and
what exactly are bad (negative) qualities

the answer is quite simple
the qualities which allow one
to behave appropriately infront
of a being higher than themselves
are good qualities
and those that don't
are bad qualities

there are of course the minions of evil demiurge
who would propagate that
there is no good and bad
but then they will also say that
there is no such thing as evolution either

only one bad/wrong/…

there is

no other

bad/wrong etc

excePT

not showing

proper

full

resPecT

to

higher

&

divine

beings

only

put their own

beingness

in

jeopardy

by not

properly

resPecTing

higher &

divine

respect

in dealing with a higher being or divine itself
one needs proper res-pect
to trigger a
proper res-ponse in one's own being
which includes the
neuroelectrics in the brain / spine
& the consciousness as a whole
more res-P-ect
= more response tingles
= more resolution in attention terms
= more restraint on devoluting impulses
= more respite from tension
= more rest from restlessness
= more results in evolution
= soul ressurection (res-sur-action)

res = rotating energy spirals
P = Pole / the axis
ect = electric charge turnings

what respect is

real respect is
simply
giving more credence to
what a higher being has said
than
self's analysis
of that statement

its best to
not analyze at all
& listen
so that the words
permeate the whole being
something
which can only happen
by ignoring
self's incessant chattering noise

posture is primary

there are many
who say to me
that they are humble
but their posture
gives them away

majority of beings these days are in
continually unhumble postures
because vedic culture
which pervaded the world
in times where there was alignment with divine
is now firmly in the background

they don't realize
it is impossible to have humble thoughts
in an unhumble posture
&
one having humble thoughts will automatically
get into a humble posture

Watch Your Posture
youtu.be/9wKLOZnzvQg

doing the do

people always seem
to be able to
do the do
when it comes to
brushing their teeth etc

but when it comes to
taking care of their soul & evolution
most cannot
do the simple do
of
using their mouths
to praise higher/divine
and
using their bodies
to serve higher/divine

it is the only way one evolves
not by thinking or internalizing

moving the mouth to praise the higher/divine
is the 'do'
only those who
do this do
with continuity
get out of the mess

simple(s)

Praise

Praise = P-Raise
Pray was just a short form of Prayze = Praise

it is either
Do-ing or P-raise-ing
one leads to hell
and other to freedom from hell

the fools believe in 'doing'
without any real rhyme or reason
the wise fix their attention on 'praising' instead

'doing' keeps on happening
despite the futility of their 'doing'
being clearly revealed through lotusocean writings

some after reading lotusocean blogs
still have the nerve to write their own blog
as if they have some other truth to share
which has not been revealed here

just doing for the sake of doing
there is no other evil
the only purpose of this doing
is avoiding praise of divine
to garner praise for the
confused depressed tormented & blind self

silence unsilenced

silence is definitely
one of the most
over-rated virtues
misrepresented as a divine attribute
through quotes like
'if speech is silver, silence is golden'
that would make krishn
speaking out bhagawadgita to arjun
a mere silvery act
silence usually just means that
some unwholesome calculation is going on within
many people can hardly ever speak
because of the incessant
& meaningless internal dialogue
such calculations may be useful in
petty politics or business or other such useless activities
but have no use in soul-evolution
in fact these calculations are
a major obstruction on the
road to heightened awareness
thats why sages of old
recommended continuous verbal repetition
of divine sounds
to rise above the selfish calculative part
which hides behind the
mask of external silence

nothing in the multiverse is really silent
to feign silence in such an existence
is a pretence
a lot is emitting out of people
by just their being/presence
without them having to actually say anything
and they cannot stop the chatter within
through any amount of external silence
no matter how much time they spend alone
how much pot they smoke
how much meditation (vipassana etc.) they do
or how much time they spend in nature
the chatter just goes on and on
the only way to curb the mind
from the unwholesome is to focus
on the wholesome
speech which praises the divine is
the only saviour from the
dark & gloomy 'sounds of silence'

prayer

there are those
who are suggesting
that prayer is done in silence
prayer comes from the term
'pray'
which in turn comes from
the term
'praise'

prayer is nothing
but
praise of higher/divine
&
this
praise is done
through
words & deeds
not silence

silence is the
mark of the insincere

all the devotees of divine
in all ages
have one thing in common
praise of divine
through word, song & deed
the more continuous
this praise is
the closer to divine they are

they are not afraid of praising divine
using their mouth and all that
the divine has given them
&
they can/will do it in any situation

they don't need
solitude or silence
for it
just like a lover doesn't mind
expressing its love
even in a crowded place

there are those
who get very anxious/defensive
at the mere mention of the fact
that
god/divine/higher has to be praised

they say 'praise' is unnecessary
& life can be lived without it
when the truth is that
even in their own life
they are always praising
either others like themselves, their own self
or those lower than themselves

majority of this world has no problems
encouraging those that don't
threaten their own ego
in simpler words
what they gno to be nothing really beyond them

its only when it comes to praising
the real higher/divine
that questions are raised
& feelings like jealousy enter the fray

in their foolish ignorance
they say 'why would higher need the praise'
well it doesn't
it is they who need to do the p(raise)
to raise themselves out of the blissless hell
they have put themselves in
through not doing it

344

emphatic repetition

everyone can perceive

at least one of the unlimited exalted qualities

of divine's manifestations

within this 3-D matrix

and that is enough

for evolution

all that is required is

emphatic verbal repetition of this perception

rising above self's inherent laziness

speech is the starting point

the body follows

mind after that

soul ...

the most natural thing

there are those
who believe in coming
down hard on their self
the self trying to discipline
its own errant unevoluting ways
is a contradiction in itself
rather than a realistic possibility

any real evolutionary discipline is not possible
without the focus
being on praise of the higher/divine

discipline is easy & automatic
for those who
learn to enjoy the bliss
which comes through doing whats natural
and nothing is more natural
than praising the higher/divine
it is an automatic impulse
only smothered by deliberate evil
inculcated over thousands of generations

all the beings in any era
ancient or recent have
only gotten to soul evolutionary discipline
through praise of divine
and those closer to it
than themselves

if one doesn't ...

if one doesn't
bow down to higher
(in terms of spiritual evolutionary status)
one gets an uncomfortable feeling
which will surely turn into
jealousy & upsetness
which will lead to incorrect behaviour
which will automatically lead to
a very quick devolutionary downfall
which leads to hells
of pain & torture
its all that simple

eye brow eye (i) bow

the upper eye brow & lid
has to bow
it is the
first step
in the important
business of
proper agreeance
jaw follows
then neck
spine after that
a body language
fast disappearing off
the face of this planet

bowing

there are many here
who think
that they can
evolve
without bowing to the real higher & divine

as they lounge on their sofas smoking away
or lie in their beds dreaming
or watch the world with puzzled befuddled eyes
they think they are learning & evolving
lotusocean has news for them
all they are doing is confusing themselves further
getting more entangled in the spiderweb
sinking further into the quicksand

the only solution –
'bowing' to higher & divine

without bowing
mental & physical
with requisite postures
there is only downfall

if they are honest enough to admit it
it is happening right before their eyes
as the world including them sinks
into deeper hell of
boredom, depression, pain & torture

most are ready to do anything for happiness
except bowing

they can bang hard on all the walls
until they realize
the simple logical truth that
there is no way out
except humbly following those who gno the way out

for 'whom/what not to bow to' read
p. 352 – the fake bows

for 'whom to bow to' read
p. 124 – how to tell between fake & real gurus

Grace

only graceful action
one can do
is sincerely
bow to divine

if that is not what one does
only other option
is disgraceful actions

and the longer one goes on
that devoluting path
more disgraceful it all gets
its all already at an insectoid level
if one puts on the TV
especially any socalled music channels

without Grace
there is no G race
or Genes on phire
racing up past speed of light
to break the matrix eggshell

the fake bows

people are ever-ready to do their
formal get-it-out-of-the-way fake bow
to established frauds like
pope, queen, dalai lama & other such charlatans
its all about bowing to the
system itself
rather than an individual

in some places
they are forced to do such bows to all elders
elder being decided by age not wisdom

in some places they do this bow
to stones & statues
ego doesn't get perturbed
especially since everyone else is doing it too

people everywhere
do this bow to
money & those who have it
in various forms

they bow to the people on stage
who bow back to them
a mutual bowing scene
which leads no-one anywhere

people are not bowing to the higher
partly because
they have wrong definitions of higher
&
mainly because of the plain evil
which takes over them with feelings like
inferiority complex & jealousy
when they do gno in their guts
it makes them not want to bow
because it will have to be a real bow
& it will have to be continuous

useful to remember that
all evil only arose from
the simple decision of
not bowing to divine

why bow ?

there are those
who ask why
i give so much
importance
to bowing

well if one doesn't bow
to high & divine
one will only get angry
with high & divine
this is but natural
& will always be the case
there is no 3rd way of being
its either bow or get upset

the result of this anger/upsetness
is really bad for one's soul
which is already caughtup in a mess
it is simply a
way to deeper hell
which doesn't seem so terrible
in written form
but is way-way worse in experiencing
its all the medieval tortures
& all the so-called modern
war tortures combined
+ much worse

guarantee

pure
intent
to
serve
guarantees
entry
into
any
world

praying for help ?

a common question
people ask

when we pray to
higher & divine
why doesn't divine help us ?

answer

because
that prayer is asking for help
not
stating one's intent to serve

a crucial difference

when there is
intent to serve
in whatever capacity one has
all the help one needs
& more
gets taken care of anyways

thank you, really ?

having received many
thank you's
lately
it is but natural to wonder
what it means

is it a Praise
or is it an uneager cop out
out of having to do anything
more substantial

is it a form of gratitude
and if so it seems
quite hollow
just 2 words
& thats it

the word itself means
than-k you or
than cut(k) you
it is more of a rude
bye bye term
than any intent of reciprocity

another western/english phrase
for concealing rudeness
in garb of politeness
thank you is just another way of saying
buzz off now

even when beings say thank you to god/divine
they just want to get rid of it
thanks for your help etc.
now can you just disappear
so that we can get on with it

thank you to higher/divine
is a cheap way
to get out of bowing

those considering 'just thankyou'
to be a first step
should gno that there is no
possibilty of any more steps
in that path
one will actually have to retract to
move forward

the most crucial thing

for anyone

wanting to improve their self/life

raise their spirit

make a soul

get out of hell & 3-d matrix

get into magick realm

get into heaven

get into higher dimensions

be with divine

...

the most crucial thing

is

to see

coming across

higher & divine

as the

greatest good fortune

to be

celebratory about it

like it is the biggest lottery

one can ever win

step 1

is seeing clearly that one has encountered higher
when one comes across higher & divine
it is not that hard to do
if one keeps one's ego in check

step 2

is seeing higher & divine
as the best thing
that can ever happen for one

step 3

unconditional service, right posture, right behaviour, right actions ...
all automatically spring from the first 2

and

the rest follows ...

think think (wink wink)

there are so many
in this world
who love to think
using their faulty little brains
powered by their unfractal genes

many have pushed thought to the limit
have encountered
confusion, frustration, insanity & suicidalness
the net result has been
a big zero

all the past wisdom and tales
make it very clear that
any evolution or rise in this multiverse
depends on praising/serving the higher/divine
not thinking

Valmiki wrote the immortal epic 'Ramayan'
by praising Raam – an incarnation of divine
not by thinking
even asuras like ravan gained power & influence
by praising/serving Shiv – a divine being

still they believe
that they will figure it all out
if they just keep reading & thinking

kundalini doesn't rise
by reading/thinking
nor does 3rd eye open by reading/thinking

all evolution happens
through actual practise
of praising/serving higher/divine

this simple fact remains
elusive despite all of their thinking
and
all of the evidence pointing towards it

realizations

centering
brings
realizations
not
thinking

blessed

so who are
the blessed

once again the
word tells it all

b-less

the ones who
are clear at all times
to
b
less
than
divine

no ego takes root
and
blessed-ness happens

terrified & ashamed

terrified & ashamed
2 words
which the world
sees in a negative light
but from lotusocean perspective
they are essential
as
no one can approach divine
properly
unless they are
terrified
of their past
& their past repeating
like a groundhog day
& of all the hellish possibilities of the future

for behaving humbly with divine
it is also logical & imperative
that they are
ashamed
of their
foolishness/actions

without this understanding
there is no humility to divine
and no getting out of hell
& hellish unsatisfactory paradigms

100% ashamed-ness required ...

there is a simple way
to get out of hell here and beyond

~

be
100%
fully
unadulterated-ly
ashamed
in front of Divine
of one's own actions
which kept one in hell

simple
but
still not many
here are doing it

'when the judgement comes
find the world in shame'

...

the MOST IMPORTANT TRiAD

HONESTY

–

SHAME

–

BOWING & SERVICE to DIVINE

real Honesty about

self's actions and not-gnoing

automatically leads to

Shame

which in turn

automatically leads to

Bowing to & Serving Divine

which

automatically leads to

PLEASURE

HEAVEN

ASCENSION to HIGHER REALMS

...

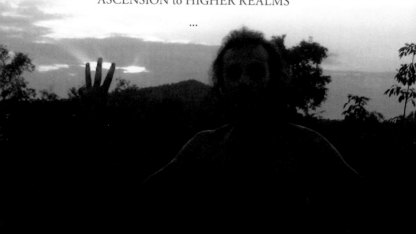

P

when P lays
its Play
when P is arty
its Party

P = the axis
of the multiversal tree
in other words
P is the Pole you spin around
what was lost is now being found

P

the letter P
is shaped as it is
to show that its 'the Axis'
the circle rotates around the central axial line

the letter P in all major languages & cultures
always represents the Axis figures
Pita (father) or Pati (husband) in Sanskrit
Ptah (the Patriarch) in Egypt
President or P resident (the central resident) in English

the fact that
P happens to be the first initial of lotusocean manifestor
PT
is just another aspect of the P-erfect fractality
all the T-turning happens around P

the AXIS

no

world

exists

without

an

AXIS

...

A

X - crossing

I-Pole

around

which

all else

Spins

...

PT

is

the

AXIS

of this

world

caPTain PT

you walk like
you gno where
you are going
you talk like
you gno what
you are doing

but the truth is
you've got no clue

you are lost
in this world &
the other ones
don't even
enter your consciousness

you are trapped and incubated

you need a navigator

captain P is a navigator
for this world
and the big beyond

he is here
to steer
the soulship home

captain P
captain P
captain PT

the one and only navigator

youtu.be/To98xS4QGvs

Phun is the real Fun

the correct spelling of

fun is Phun

as in

Phee Phi Pho Phum

one has to

get Phi (heart of gold)

to get Phun

it all once again revolves around P

haPPy

there is a reason for everything

and there is a reason why

haPPy has

2 Ps in it

P-REACH

some say that

i PREACH too much

they forget

its their job to

REACH P

not mine

Prefer

it is
always
Preferable
to
refer
to
P
(the axis)
instead
of
self-refer
as
many
are suggesting
or
automatically do

Present

the
Present
is
a
Present
re-sent
from
P
which
not
many
treasure
the way
they should

avoid

a-void

P

the

Axis

&

be

left

with

the

void

which

nothing

else

can

fill

simples

judgement day

there are many who
hold the belief
that they will be judged
on a day
called
judgement day

well they are right
only discrepancy being
the day
is already here
and
all are being judged
right now
everyday

that's what
i am here for
lotusocean
tells you the results

EVENT HORIZON

PT – LotusOcean
is
the Real & Only
Event Horizon
for
whosoever
anywhere
comes
across
any of it

that is the
PoinT
of
no return

how
anyone
responds to
this
encounter
is
the
only
action
which decides
their
Phuture
...
Nothing
Else
Matters
...

HIGHER and DIVINE

The
3 Pillars
of Right Behaviour

Praise

Bow

Serve

Being-ness

Praising Bowing & Serving – the Most Natural Sequence

when one comes across

a Praiseworthy being

more

higher & divine

than oneself

it is natural

to

Praise

repetition of that Praise

naturally leads to

Bowing

repetition of that Bowing

naturally leads to

Serving

and

this sequence

lifts one out of any hell

into

higher consciousness

&

higher realms

...

PT's world

people ask
what kind of world
would it be
if my precepts were followed ?

the answer is
it would be
a world
without
pollution
disease
depression
&
devolution

it would be
a world
which would be
advanced in
the real sense
of the word
from all perspectives

an ever-evoluting
paradise

which would

be a model

for the

rest of the galaxy

&

multiverse

PT's World

youtu.be/4lu60lt0v4Y

youtu.be/3KstfMoXZZQ

who am I ~ the PT avatar

many ask

who am I

funny since

they cannot really answer

who they are

they ask but its clear

they really don't want to gno

deep down there is an inkling

the reality might be too much to handle

for those who feel/think they can handle it

here are some highlights

of the PT avatar

can't cover all the aspects

simply because they are infinite –

I am Harry Potter – Hari Putra

meaning Emanation of Hari

'Hari' – 'the stealer of hearts' being one the many names for Divine

who lives under the stairs (literally)

& has a scar above the right eye

who wields many magic wands

& has always topped at the University of Magic

The 888 Story <u>youtu.be/rGXuIve3SXA</u>

I am Flash Gordon
who rescues humanity
from Galactic techno-evilarchy
through real Flash Power

I am Captain Kirk
who steers this planets course
from the Bridge

I am the Alpha & the Omega

I am the real ॐ (Aeioum)

ॐ CropCircle on 7.7.7 ~ Prashant Trivedi
youtu.be/mXcgPhkf8B4

Aeioumonics ~ Dimension hopping ~ PT
https://youtu.be/N0KQy-ERp40

ALL I See

is

a Great Big Sea

You are all just rivers flowing into this big big Sea

Sea that is Me

PoinT inside Time which is All the Time ~ PT
youtu.be/Dqpt4sWcj-U